FACT AND FAITH
IN THE
KERYGMA OF TODAY

PAUL ALTHAUS

FACT AND FAITH
IN THE
KERYGMA OF TODAY

Translated by
DAVID CAIRNS

MUHLENBERG PRESS
PHILADELPHIA

A translation of *Das sogenannte Kerygma und der historische Jesus; Zur Kritik der heutigen Kerygma-Theologie*, by Paul Althaus, published by Carl Bertelsmann Verlag, Gütersloh, 1958, as VOL. XLVIII in the series Beiträge zur Förderung christlicher Theologie.

ENGLISH EDITION
First published 1959

Library of Congress Catalogue Number 60-7473

PRINTED IN GREAT BRITAIN FOR OLIVER AND BOYD LTD
BY ROBERT CUNNINGHAM AND SONS LTD, LONGBANK WORKS, ALVA

Foreword

RUDOLF BULTMANN's theological project has roused interest and activity among theologians and church-men chiefly because of his programme of "demy-thologising" and "existential interpretation." But there is another aspect of his theology closely connected with the existentialist approach, which is not less stimulating. I refer to his severance of the *kerygma* and consequently of Christology from the problem of the historical Jesus. The following discussion deals with his views on this point. There is all the more prospect of entering into a fruitful discussion with Rudolf Bultmann and Friedrich Gogarten, who has come to his support on this issue; because the doubts and questions which move me are also giving concern to theologians who stand near to Bultmann, like Günther Bornkamm and Ernst Käsemann. Bornkamm's book on Jesus (1956), has carried the discussion a con-siderable way beyond Bultmann's thesis.

The last section of my work does not deal with the relationship of the *kerygma* to the historical Jesus, but with Bultmann's "demythologised" Christology. (I have given my views on Bultmann's programme in general in the *Theologische Literaturzeitung*, 1942, pp. 337-44.)

No small part of the following discussion deals with criticisms and questions which in the last five years have been addressed to Bultmann from other quarters also. In addition to the theologians already named, I refer to G. Gloege, *Mythologie und Luthertum*, Berlin 1952; to the volume *Zur Entmythologisierung. Ein Wort lutherischer Theologie*, Munich 1952 (E. Ellwein, E. Kinder and W. Künneth), and to Hermann Diem, *Dogmatik*, Munich

5

1955, pp. 76-128, English translation by Harold Knight, *Dogmatics*, Edinburgh 1959, pp. 83-143. I consciously underline, by means of many references and quotations, the consensus which, in spite of other theological differences, is here shown.

It was not until I had concluded my work that I became acquainted with the following essays dealing with the same theme, and in partial agreement with my own. It was too late to refer to them, but I wish to name them here: H. Engelland, "Gewissheit um Jesus von Nazareth," in *Theologische Literaturzeitung*, 1954, pp. 65-74; O. Michel, "Der 'historische Jesus' und das theologische Gewissheitsproblem," in *Evangelische Theologie*, xv (1955), pp. 349-63; N. A. Dahl, "Der historische Jesus als geschichtswissenschaftliches und theologisches Problem," in *Kerygma und Dogma*, 1955, pp. 104-32. The same is true of Gustaf Wingren's important book, *Die Methodenfrage der Theologie*, Göttingen 1957, esp. pp. 126ff., "Bultmanns Deutung des Kerygmas." I am delighted to find myself in agreement with him in decisively important matters.

The main contents of this book were delivered by me as guest lecturer in the Universities of Tübingen and East Berlin in January-October 1957, and at the Hanover Whitsun Conference in June 1957.

Erlangen, *November 1957*

Contents

List of Abbreviations and of Works Cited

ALTHAUS, PAUL. *Die Christliche Wahrheit.* Gütersloh 1949.
— *Die Wahrheit des Kirchlichen Osterglaubens.* Gütersloh 1941.
— *Grundriss der Dogmatik.* Erlangen 1929.
— *Theologische Aufsätze.* Gütersloh 1935.
BARTH, KARL. *Die Auferstehung der Toten.* Munich 1926.
— *Kirchliche Dogmatik,* VOL. III, PT II. Zollikon-Zürich 1948.
    Eng. trans. by Harold Knight and R. H. Fuller, *Church Dogmatics,* VOL. III, PT II, Edinburgh 1960.
BORNKAMM, GÜNTHER. *Jesus von Nazareth.* Stuttgart 1956.
— "Mythos und Evangelium," in *Theologische Existenz heute,* n.s. XXVI, 1951.
BRUNNER, E. *Das Ewige als Zukunft und Gegenwart.* Zürich 1953.
    Eng. trans. by Harold Knight, *Eternal Hope.* London 1954.
BULTMANN, RUDOLF. *Der Begriff der Offenbarung im Neuen Testament.* Tübingen 1929.
— *Die Christliche Hoffnung und das Problem der Entmythologisierung.* Stuttgart 1954.
— *Glauben und Verstehen.* Tübingen 1933.
— *Jesus.* Berlin 1926.
— *Kerygma und Mythos.* Hamburg 1948.
— *Offenbarung und Heilsgeschehen.* Munich 1941.
— *Theologie des Neuen Testaments.* Tübingen 1948.
— "Zur Frage der Christologie," in *Zwischen den Zeiten.* Munich 1927.
BURI, FRITZ. *Die Bedeutung der neutestamentlichen Eschatologie in der neueren protestantischen Theologie.* Zürich 1935.
Das Neue Testament Deutsch. 8th edn. VOL. III. Göttingen 1958.
DIBELIUS, MARTIN. *Die Formgeschichte des Evangeliums.* Tübingen 1919.

DIEM, HERMANN. *Theologie als Kirchliche Wissenschaft*, BD II, *Dogmatik*. Munich 1955. Eng. trans. by Harold Knight, *Dogmatics*. Edinburgh 1959.

ELLWEIN, E., KINDER, E., and KÜNNETH, W. *Zur Entmythologisierung. Ein Wort lutherischer Theologie*. Munich 1952.

FICHTE, J. G. *Anweisung zum seligen Leben*. In *Werke in Auswahl*, ed. F. Medicus. Leipzig 1908-11. VOL. V. Eng. trans. by W. Smith, *The Way towards the Blessed Life*, in *Popular Works*. VOL. II. London 1849.

GLOEGE, G. *Mythologie und Luthertum*. Berlin 1952.

GOGARTEN, FRIEDRICH. *Entmythologisierung und Kirche*. 2nd edn. Stuttgart 1954.

— *Verhängnis und Hoffnung der Neuzeit*. Stuttgart 1953.

— *Was ist Christentum?* Stuttgart 1956.

GRASS, H. *Ostergeschehen und Osterberichte*. Göttingen 1956.

HEIM, KARL. *Leitfaden der Dogmatik*. 3rd edn. Halle 1923.

HERRMANN, WILHELM. *Der Verkehr des Christen mit Gott*. 5th and 6th edns. Stuttgart and Berlin 1908.

— *Dogmatik*. Gotha and Stuttgart 1925.

HIRSCH, EMMANUEL. *Die Auferstehungsgeschichten und der christliche Glaube*. Tübingen 1940.

KÄHLER, MARTIN. *Historische Jesus = Der sogenannte historische Jesus und der geschichtliche biblische Christus*. Leipzig 1892.

— *Wissenschaft der christlichen Lehre*. 3rd edn. Leipzig 1905.

KÄSEMANN, ERNST. "Das Problem des historischen Jesus," in *Z. Th. K.*, LI, 1954.

— "Probleme der neutestamentlichen Arbeit in Deutschland," in *Die Freiheit des Evangeliums und die Ordnung der Gesellschaft*. Beiträge zur Evangelischen Theologie, BD XV, 1952.

KINDER, ERNST. *Das neuzeitliche Geschichtsdenken und die Theologie. Antwort an Fr. Gogarten*. Luthertum, Heft XII. Berlin 1954. See also under ELLWEIN, E.

Kittel = *Theologisches Wörterbuch zum Neuen Testament*, ed. G. Kittel. VOL. IV. Stuttgart 1933.

KÜNNETH, W. See under ELLWEIN, E.

LUTHER, MARTIN. *Werke. Kritische Gesamtausgabe*, ed. J. C. F. Knaake. Weimar 1883. VOL. XXIII.

MUNDLE, W. *Der Glaube an Christus und der historische Zweifel.* Metzingen 1950.

RITSCHL, ALBRECHT. *Rechtfertigung und Versöhnung.* 4th edn. Bonn 1910.

STAUFFER, E. *Jesus: Gestalt und Geschichte.* Bern 1957.

STEINBACH, E. *Mythos und Geschichte.* Tübingen 1951.

Th. Lz. = *Theologische Literaturzeitung.*

TROELTSCH, ERNST. *Die Bedeutung der Geschichtlichkeit Jesu für den Glauben.* Tübingen 1911.

Z. Th. K. = *Zeitschrift für Theologie und Kirche.*

1

Introduction

CHRISTOLOGY is the theological doctrine of Jesus Christ the historical and exalted Saviour, the doctrine of His person and history. That is, in Christology the believer in Jesus Christ reflects theologically on the basis and content of his knowledge of Christ. We can accordingly speak of Christology only where Christian faith is unambiguously understood as faith in the person of Jesus Christ, i.e. where Jesus Christ in person is acknowledged as the revelation, as the truth disclosed to humanity by God, as salvation.

German idealist philosophy too ascribes to the historical person of Jesus an important place. But it makes a distinction between the saving truth and His person. He has His unique position and significance as the one who first brought the deepest knowledge to mankind, and embodied it in His person. In the thought of J. G. Fichte it is the knowledge of the "absolute unity of human existence with the Divine Existence": that is "the deepest knowledge to which man can attain. It was never attained before Jesus came." That He had it, is a great, "a prodigious miracle." And in virtue of it, Jesus is "the only-begotten and first-begotten Son of God," and "all times which are able to understand Him, will acknowledge Him as such."[1]

[1] *Anweisung zum seligen Leben*, 1806, reprinted in *Werke in Auswahl*, ed. F. Medicus, Leipzig 1908-11, VOL. V, pp. 195ff.; Eng. trans. *The Way towards the Blessed Life*, by W. Smith, in *Popular Works*, VOL. II, London 1849, pp. 389ff.

"Until the end of time all men of understanding will bow humbly before this Jesus of Nazareth, and the more worthy they themselves are, the more will they acknowledge the superlative glory of this great phenomenon." All this is true of Jesus in virtue of His *historical* significance. But Christianity, rightly understood, is not *essentially* bound to Him. He was the way to the truth, but the way is not the *truth* itself. "If a man is really united to God, and has entered into Him, it matters not at all by which way he came to Him, and it would be a very profitless and perverse occupation, if instead of living in the reality, we were continually to repeat the memory of the way to it."[2]

This distinction between the way and the reality, or between the thing and the symbol for it, is characteristic of the whole idealistic philosophy. It has also entered into theology in so far as this has been influenced by philosophical idealism. Thus D. F. Strauss distinguishes between "the idea of Christ"—i.e. humanity's oneness with God—and the person of Jesus; in like manner, A. E. Biedermann and Alexander Schweizer distinguish between the Christian principle and the person of Jesus, between the historical and the ideal Christ. Jesus is the "historical redeemer," says Biedermann, "as the historical revelation of the principle of redemption," but we must distinguish the "essential content" of Church Christology from the historical person of Jesus.

The distinction between the Christ-principle and the person of Jesus among theologians influenced by Hegel was not due solely to idealistic influences; there was also a historical-critical factor—doubt as to the historicity of the picture of Jesus given by the gospels. This was true also of Ernst Troeltsch. He did not, indeed, use the idealistic formulae for the principle of Christianity; but he also knew the "Christian idea," the "ever new redemp-

[2] *Op. cit.*, p. 197; Eng. trans., p. 391.

14

tion through the knowledge of God which is given to faith," and did not regard faith as unconditionally tied to the person of Jesus. There is no theologically demonstrable necessity for Christianity's need of the person of Jesus. He is necessary as a cult-symbol, merely to fulfil some law of social psychology. Such a symbol does not need to have been a historical figure.[3] In none of these cases can we speak of Christology in the strict sense of the word. For here we can say of faith that it is faith which believes in relation to Jesus, through Jesus, like Jesus, yes, even for Jesus's sake, but it is no longer faith *in* Jesus.

The dissolution of Christology can, however, simply arise from the fact that doubts have arisen as to whether the real Jesus of the gospels is able to support a Christology in the previously accepted sense of the term. In this case we do not start from a preconceived notion of the gospel as idea, like the idealist philosophers and theologians, but from the crisis in relation to the person of Jesus. And then, in the second place, we look for the concept, the idea, for which, in spite of all, the historical person of Jesus must be a "symbol." This is true of the Bern school of Martin Werner, and perhaps of his pupil Fritz Buri in Basel, who at the same time sympathises with the existentialist philosophy of Jaspers. This school has been influenced by Albert Schweitzer, and its fundamental concepts are familiar. It starts from the radically eschatological interpretation of Jesus. Jesus's own faith—that in His own lifetime, or through death and resurrection, He would immediately bring in the Kingdom—was disappointed. The immediately expected Parousia never came. This failure called in question, declared bankrupt, and finally discredited not only Jesus's messianic expectation, but His whole self-consciousness. The dogmatic Christology of the early Church is interpreted as a sub-

[3] E. Troeltsch, *Die Bedeutung der Geschichtlichkeit Jesu für den Glauben*, Tübingen 1911.

stitute for the Parousia which never happened, and as a piece of mythology. Intellectual honesty demands that we give it up. In any case, it has nothing to do with the real Christ. What is left? "The concept of Christ"—but that is an expression for "Reverence for the mystery of creation as a principle of action from the motive of reverence for life." "Christ" is only a symbol for the "Possibility latent in creation for the realisation of actual significance in the midst of the irrationality of the world" through "active and passive reverence for life"[4]; "We cannot with historical or dogmatic literalism repeat the confession of the primitive Church: 'Jesus is the Christ'; but we can, in terms of our self-understanding as existence, see in it the revelation of God as the Redeemer, and it becomes to us a legitimate mythological symbol of existence as grace."[5] Moreover the eschatological Christology of the New Testament is, we are told, "of special significance for an existential Christology." But neither in this case can we speak any longer of faith in the historical Jesus Christ. Although Buri claims the title "Christology" for his reflexions, in fact they mean the dissolution of Christology.

In general we must make two objections to the Bern school. First the non-occurrence of the Parousia, which is here dramatised as being of absolutely decisive importance, clearly did not have for the primitive Christian community anything like the central significance that is now being ascribed to it.[6] Second; the development of Christology and soteriology was not a substitute for an eschatology which had become questionable. This development depended rather on the presence of Jesus

---

[4] F. Buri, *Die Bedeutung der neutestamentlichen Eschatologie in der neueren protestantischen Theologie*, Zürich 1935, pp. 170ff.

[5] Id., *Theologie der Existenz*, Bern 1954, pp. 90ff., "Christologie der Existenz."

[6] Cf. also E. Brunner, *Das Ewige als Zukunft und Gegenwart*, Zürich 1953, p. 141; Eng. trans. *Eternal Hope*, by Harold Knight, London 1954, p. 128.

Christ and the salvation He brought with Him, a presence which was certified by the resurrection of Christ, but which had been emphasised even in Jesus's own preaching.

Very different from all these types of symbolical interpretation of Jesus and the gospel, and in sharp opposition to them, is the contemporary *kerygma* theology. Bultmann speaks of "a decisive action of God in Christ" and of "an eschatological salvation-event in Him." His intention is to do full justice to "the paradox of New Testament preaching," i.e. the paradox that God's eschatological vicegerent is a concrete historical man, that God's eschatological action is fulfilled in a human destiny.[7] "The revelation consists in nothing else than the fact of Jesus Christ"—thus Bultmann interprets the consensus of the New Testament[8]; and he affirms it also as his own theological confession. Here saving truth and salvation does not consist in something of which Christ was only the bearer or symbol, but clearly in Himself, in His person, His story. From the standpoint of the abovementioned idealistic distinction between principle and person, Bultmann's assertion that God has acted decisively in Christ must unquestionably be regarded as mythology, and not less so from the standpoint of contemporary existentialist philosophy. Here lies also the clear difference between Bultmann and the older liberal theology. He reproaches it with having "deprived the New Testament preaching of its *kerygma*-character," because it does not speak of the person of Jesus as "the decisive salvation-event," nor yet of "a decisive action of God in Christ."[9]

But now we must ask whether Bultmann, in his attempt to vindicate theologically the kerygmatic character of the New Testament message, really gives the *kerygma* about Jesus Christ the same character which the New Testament

---

[7] R. Bultmann, *Offenbarung und Heilsgeschehen*, Munich 1941, p. 68.

[8] *Der Begriff der Offenbarung im Neuen Testament*, Tübingen 1929, p. 25.

[9] *Offenbarung und Heilsgeschehen*, p. 40.

assigns to it. We call Bultmann's theology "kerygmatic theology" because it makes the apostolic *kerygma* the basis of theology in such a manner that the foundation of the *kerygma* itself in the figure and story of the historical Jesus is overshadowed and left out of account as having no theological significance. Thus, though this theology is very far removed from the reduction of the historical Jesus to a symbol, a reduction characteristic of idealistic philosophy and theology, none the less, there is an unmistakable danger that here also the theological interest of "the historical Jesus" may be undervalued. It is true that a distinction is no longer drawn between the Christ-principle and Christ's person, the latter being declared of merely relative importance in comparison with the former. But the *kerygma* and the historical Jesus are torn apart, and the importance of the latter is minimised in comparison with the *kerygma*.

2

Martin Kähler and *Kerygma* Christology

PRESENT-DAY *kerygma* theology considers itself to be a
resumption and justification of theses which were
first propounded in 1892 by Martin Kähler in his
famous book, *Der sogenannte historische Jesus und der geschichtliche biblische Christus.*[1] It is no accident that this
book was recently (1956) republished. In it Martin
Kähler protests against the contemporary "Lives of
Jesus," and particularly against the kind of historical
relativism, which claimed by the use of scientific historical
method to resuscitate the so-called "historical Jesus," and
to offer this to the Christian Church as the ground and
object of its faith. This procedure, Kähler asserts, is an
error both from the standpoint of faith and from that of
historical scholarship. "My intention is not merely to
defend faith's independence of theology, but also, very
definitely, to establish the right scholarly method."[2] In
relation to faith, the claim of the historian that he alone
can provide faith with its object and ground, is an assault
upon faith's independence of theology. Faith in this
manner becomes dependent on the scholars, and grows
perplexed in view of the difference of their results. The
ground and object of faith, Jesus Christ, must be immediately accessible to every Christian. "Faith must not
be dependent on the uncertain conclusions about a re-
putedly reliable picture of Jesus which is tortured out of

---

[1] *Der sogenannte historische Jesus und der geschichtliche biblische Christus,*
henceforth cited as *Historische Jesus,* Leipzig 1892.   [2] *Op. cit.,* p. 96.

the sources by the methods of recently-developed historical investigation. . . . For in relation to the Christ in whom
we have the duty and the privilege of believing, the most
learned theologian must be no better off and no worse off
than the simplest Christian."[3] "How can Jesus Christ be
the proper object of the faith of all Christians, if what and
who He really was can only be established by a com-
plicated investigation, and if it is only the science of our
time which has shown itself equal to this task. How can
this uncertain deposit left by the corrosive acids of
criticism (i.e. the historical Jesus), how can this figure
whom now for the first time scholarship can discern
through the mists of antiquity, be the object of the
faith of all Christians? And moreover, how can it have
been so in the past in spite of this veil which only our
contemporaries have had the good fortune to strip away?"[4]
"Historical facts which can be established only by science
cannot *as such* be experiences of faith . . ."[5] Thus, "it is
today the task of the dogmatic theologian, as representa-
tive of the simple faith of Christians, to set limits to the
papal pretensions of the historians."[6] This is the religious,
the evangelical significance of Kähler's protest. He was
resisting the encroachments of historical scholarship upon
the rights of simple Christian men.

At the same time Kähler shows that in point of scholarship the "Lives of Jesus," and "the search for the historical
Jesus," were following a blind alley. For of the "Lives"
it is true that "It is for the most part these gentlemen's
own views which they see reflected in Jesus."[7] The des-
criptive biographer is a concealed dogmatic theologian.
But leaving out of account this characteristic of the
artistic and imaginative attempts to produce a "Life" of
Jesus, there is one fundamental observation which must
be made. This Jesus, whose picture is to be reconstructed

---

[3] *Op. cit.*, p. 73.   [4] *Op. cit.*, pp. 3ff.   [5] *Op. cit.*, p. 74.
[6] *Op. cit.*, p. 73.   [7] *Op. cit.*. p. 57.

from the tradition by means of historical investigation, is not really the historic[8] Jesus at all. It is in his work (*Werk*) that a person is historic. But Jesus's achievement is the faith of His disciples in Him, and the confession of this faith.[9] But this faith was not elicited from the disciples by the historical Jesus "as He lived and walked," but only by Jesus the risen and living Lord. "Without this we would know nothing at all of Him." According to the documentary sources the certainty of the disciples and apostles that "Christ is Lord" is inseparable from the other certainty that He is the living crucified and risen Saviour."[10] But this risen Saviour is not "the historical Jesus *behind* the gospels, rather is He the Christ of the apostolic preaching, the Christ *of the whole New Testament. The real Christ is the preached Christ*, and the preached Christ is the Christ of faith."[11] Only the whole biblical Christ is the real, historic, Christ. The biblical Christ is the only historically credible and accessible Christ.[12]

The search for the "historical Jesus" also contradicts the character of the gospels, and vice versa; the latter supports the thesis that the real Christ is the Christ who is preached, the risen, living Christ. The gospels are not in the least like historical sources, as the historian understands the term; the evangelists are "preachers"—John

[8] *Translator's note*: At this point the translator is in a real difficulty. Where the English language has only two words: "history," "historical," the German language has four: "Geschichte," "geschichtlich"; "Historie," "historisch." Kähler introduced a special sense of the first pair of terms, whose sense will become clear in the following pages. Bultmann has taken over Kähler's terminology, not without a sinister change of meaning. Further, Bultmann is not consistent in the use of his own terminology. The translator must use the term "history" for both "Geschichte" and "Historie." But where it is clear that the special sense of "geschichtlich" intended by Kähler and the writers like Gogarten and Bultmann who have more or less followed him, is meant, the English word "historic" will be used; and the reader is warned that this word is to be read in this special sense, which is rather different from the usual meaning of the word in English.

[9] Kähler, *Historische Jesus*, p. 63.   [10] *Op. cit.*, p. 64.
[11] *Op. cit.*, p. 66.   [12] *Op. cit.*, p. 96.

(xx.31) acknowledges openly that this is true of himself, and "the other evangelists are in truth, preachers no less than he."[13] The reports of the gospels, which at the first glance are so different from the "dogmatic" utterances of the epistles about Christ, show in fact "the same dogmatic characteristics" as do the messianic speeches of Acts; "they are sermons about the messianic character of the Crucified."[14] In particular, with regard to facts about the end of Jesus's life, "that is, for its authentic content, for its permanent value, there *can* be no historical sources, but only witness and faith."[15] The light of Easter shines on the picture of Jesus given in the gospels, whose writers see that the Lord that walked on earth is one with the risen and living Saviour. "The portrayal given by the gospels does not merely find its climax in the Easter story; from the beginning its perspective is the perspective of Easter."[16]

In Kähler's time this interpretation of the gospels met with lively opposition; it was asserted to be an intolerable expression of historical scepticism. But in our century historical investigation of the gospels has of itself been led to confirm Kähler's thesis, through the insights gained by form-criticism. From the time of Martin Dibelius's *Formgeschichte des Evangeliums*[17] Kähler's fundamental concepts were confirmed and given more pointed expression by exact form-critical investigation of the gospels. It was realised that the Easter faith of the Church was an important contributive factor and a permeating influence in the formation of the account of Jesus given in the gospels. The gospels are account and interpretation in one, and interpretation in the light of Easter. As such they are full of the Christology of the Church, and mirror its development and its differences. In this way the picture of the historical Jesus is obscured and hidden, and is consequently relatively unrecognisable. We have Jesus only in

[13] *Op. cit.*, pp. 8off.   [14] *Op. cit.*, pp. 82ff.   [15] *Op. cit.*, p. 95.
[16] *Op. cit.*, p. 108.   [17] Tübingen 1919.

22

the faith of the Church, in the apostolic preaching about Him, i.e. in the "kerygma." To try to go behind this to a "historical Jesus" is historically a hopeless and perverse undertaking. The primitive Christian Church could not, and did not try to "sever the history of Jesus from its own history." and therefore it "neither wished, nor was able to abstract from its Easter faith and distinguish between the earthly and the exalted Lord." Thus it "proclaimed that an inquiry directed to the historical Jesus alone seemed to it an abstraction."[18] In like manner, knowing these facts, theology today must not inquire about Jesus Christ, except in so far as it listens to the apostolic preaching. Thus dogmatic theologians evaluated the knowledge gained by form-critical methods; in the person of Rudolf Bultmann historical inquiry and dogmatics are linked together in personal union.

Now in this thesis that we must make our theological beginning with the *kerygma*, as the ultimate datum accessible to faith in Christ, and that we must not go behind it, there is doubtless one real insight that we must never again lose. And that is the knowledge that there is not, and that there never has been, any other gospel than the authentic gospel *about* Jesus Christ. To attempt to get behind "Christ" to "Jesus," as theological liberalism did, is utterly out of the question. Today there is almost complete agreement on this point among all schools of theology. Research carried out principally by liberal theologians—research of a historical character uninfluenced by dogmatic considerations—has itself led to the conclusion that the gospel did not come into being until Easter.

And yet, certain though it may be that dogmatic theology is forbidden to try to get behind the *kerygma* and the Christ proclaimed by it, the question still arises whether in another sense theology must not go behind

[18] E. Käsemann, "Das Problem des historischen Jesus," in *Zeitschrift für Theologie und Kirche*, henceforth cited as *Z. Th. K.*, LI (1954), p. 133.

the *kerygma*; i.e. whether it must not inquire what is *the relation of the kerygma to the history*, about which it informs us, and to which it bears witness.[19]

We cannot naïvely stop our ears to the question whether we are not, in the apostolic *kerygma*, dealing with a *myth*, the picture of a Saviour which, as so often happens in religion, is a wish-fulfilment arising from the longings of the human heart. Critical inquiry has shown to how large an extent primitive Christology applied to Jesus Saviour-names and concepts lying ready to hand both in Jewish and Gentile tradition; this is evident not only in the epistles but in the gospels. The language of Christ-ology is to a great extent mythological. Is the thing itself not also a myth? We cannot evade this question. This means, however, that we cannot accept the apostolic *kerygma* in this sense as an ultimate datum for theology. To use Günther Bornkamm's language, "We must look for the history in the *kerygma*."[20] Only thus shall we do justice to the fact that in the New Testament we have not only the thoroughly kerygmatic apostolic writings, but before them, and along with them, the gospels, which indeed owe something of their form to the *kerygma*, but are relatively distinguished from the epistles by their narrative character. The Church did not only proclaim the gospel and listen to its proclamation, but also re-peated and preserved the remembered tradition of Jesus's words and His story, interpreted, of course, in the light of Easter. This fact, that alongside the epistles stand the gospels, with their narratives of the story of Jesus which preceded the first Easter, distinguishes the gospel sharply from a myth. In its own way it anchors the Easter *kerygma* in history, certainly quite differently from the way in which a modern historian would do so,[21] but quite

[19] Cf. P. Althaus, *Die Christliche Wahrheit*, Gütersloh 1949, p. 15.
[20] G. Bornkamm, *Jesus von Nazareth*, Stuttgart 1956, p. 18.
[21] See *op. cit.*, p. 20.

24

49660

clearly enough. In so far as it does so, the gospels are
historical sources, admittedly not solely, and not primarily, but secondarily. While it was necessary for Martin
Kähler in his day, in reaction against the writers of the
"lives" of Jesus, to emphasise the fact that the gospels
are not *primarily* sources, but testimonies of faith, today
the emphasis must be placed elsewhere; the gospels are
also narratives and sources. Accordingly the retrospective
historical question as to the historical basis of the *kerygma*
is unexceptionable and theologically legitimate. By the
character of the gospels, the New Testament itself invites
us to such historical reflexion.[22]

Kähler himself did not refuse to ask questions of a
historical character. He does not evade the question
whether the picture which the gospels give of Jesus may
not be wholly legendary, a pious fiction. He answers it
thus: "All the biblical descriptions produce the irresistible
impression of the completest reality. One might venture
to predict how Jesus would have acted in this situation or
in that—indeed, even what He would have said. There-

---

[22] In *Z. Th. K.*, LI (1954), p. 141, Käsemann says: "Nor can we deny the
identity of the exalted Lord with the incarnate Lord without falling into
docetism, and depriving ourselves of the possibility of distinguishing the
Easter faith of the Church from a myth." Elsewhere ("Probleme der
neutestamentlichen Arbeit in Deutschland," in *Die Freiheit des Evangeliums
und die Ordnung der Gesellschaft*, Beiträge zur evangelischen Theologie, BD XV,
1952, cited in Diem, *Dogmatik*, p. 78f., Eng. trans. p. 85f.) Käsemann says:
"The whole New Testament claims that the disciples at Easter did not
recognise any heavenly being, much less an abstract content of knowledge
like dogmatic propositions, but Jesus Himself. The Christ who since the first
Easter has been the object of faith and the theme of preaching, is continuous
with the so-called historical Jesus, a continuity without which, faith and
preaching, in the opinion of the primitive Christian community, would be
meaningless. To apprehend with certainty this continuity is an inescapable
theological necessity. A theology which, from historical scepticism or on
strange dogmatic grounds, attempted to surrender this continuity, would not
be worthy of the name." Käsemann rejects the proposal of a particular theology "to veto on theological grounds the attempt to ask what happened before
the Easter event. To make a virtue out of necessity is much too facile a
solution to give us any satisfaction."

25

fore we can have converse with this Jesus, and need for this purpose nothing more than the biblical representation.[23] The picture of Him, so full of life, so singularly beyond the power of invention, is not the idealising creation of a human mind; here His own being has left its imperishable impression."[24] "He Himself is the author of this picture. . . . Out of these fragmentary traditions, these uncomprehended memories, these descriptions coloured by the peculiarities of the writer, these confessions of the heart, and these sermons about His power to save, there looks at us the lifelike, coherent, and repeatedly recognisable picture of a Man. Thus one must come to the conclusion that here the man in His incomparable and mighty personality, with His unparalleled actions and experiences, culminating in the appearances after His Resurrection, has etched His picture into the mind and memory of His followers so sharply and so deeply, that it could neither be erased nor distorted."[25] In the same vein Kähler writes: "His person has drawn itself in the Biblical narratives, as the singularity, so far beyond the power of invention, of this living portrait shows by the way in which it arrests our attention, and immediately convinces us of its authenticity. Although Jesus . . . appears quite incomparable, His whole figure is perfectly clear and real, these traits themselves are not portrayed merely in negative and superlative terms; and thus we may be sure that this picture is not the product of poetic invention. His contemporaries, by their own express and involuntary confession, did not understand Him and His life. If, in spite of this, the sources agree on all sides to give us a consistent picture of Him, we may conclude that its features and character are not the creation of the inadequate comprehension of His contemporaries. We get the overwhelming impression of His

[23] Kähler, *Historische Jesus*, p. 78.
[24] *Op. cit.*, p. 79.   [25] *Op. cit.*, pp. 87, 89.

person as a self-coherent, authentic, and quite singular whole," of a "clearly defined personality."[26] All these statements contain unquestionably historical judgments, though perhaps of a prescientific kind. We are not dealing here purely with judgments of faith. Kähler's opinion is rather that everyone who has a sense for reality will agree with his judgments. He declares himself, that "to receive the impression of fullest reality" a man must have a mind that "has enough modesty and patience, to live, as it were, with the person, and enter sympathetically into its particular life."[27] In order to do this faith is not essential; such a sense is independent of faith, and can precede it—though certainly historical judgments of this kind become even more clear and certain through the believer's intimacy with the picture of Jesus. Thus Martin Kähler himself asks the retrospective question, and makes historical judgments, and directs us to seek for historical assurance.

But it is just this search which is forbidden today by those who in other respects appeal to Kähler's fundamental thesis, and seek to renew it in the contemporary situation. I refer to the *kerygma*-theology of R. Bultmann with which F. Gogarten has declared himself in fundamental agreement.

Here Kähler's proposition that we cannot theologically and dogmatically go behind the *kerygma*, is affirmed. But in contrast with Kähler, the retrospective question as to the historical ground of the *kerygma* is also vetoed. Here we have to do with an outlook indifferent to, or rather hostile to, history.

Bultmann forbids faith and theology to ask what is the reality of Easter, the Easter event which stands behind the Easter *kerygma*. "Christ, the crucified and risen, meets us in the word of preaching and nowhere else. It would

[26] *Wissenschaft der christlichen Lehre,* 3rd edn. Leipzig 1905, p. 323.
[27] *Historische Jesus,* p. 78, n. 1.

27

be an error if we were here to ask what was the historical origin of the message, as if this origin could justify its legitimacy. That would mean that we were wishing to establish faith in God's word by means of historical investigation. The word of preaching meets us as God's word, and when we confront it we cannot ask any questions as to its legitimacy. Rather does it ask us whether we are willing to believe or not."[28] "The Christian Easter faith is not interested in the historical question. To ask retrospectively whether the claim of the apostolic preaching is historically justified, is tantamount to rejecting it. This question must be exchanged for the question which the questioner has to put to himself. Will he acknowledge the lordship of Christ?, a lordship which puts to him the decisive question, 'How will he understand his own being?'" The event of salvation is "nowhere present except in the word of preaching which addresses us. A report of memory, i.e. a report referring to a past happening, cannot make the salvation event visible."[29] The last sentence is certainly true. But what of the previous ones? The quotations from *Offenbarung und Heilsgeschehen* reproduce Bultmann's own theological convictions. The sentences from *Theologie des Neuen Testaments* occur within the exposition of the Pauline theology. Thus it is implied that this is what the apostle thinks. But in truth it is not Paul who is speaking here, but Bultmann. When he is dealing with the subject of the Easter *kerygma*, Paul has no thought of vetoing the question of historical legitimation. He expressly appeals to a tradition (*Paradosis*) which he has received, of course from the primitive Church (I Cor. xv.3), and emphatically and earnestly appeals to witnesses to whom appearances of the Lord were granted— *witnesses* of the fact of which preaching speaks. In his exposition of I Cor. xv. Karl Barth tried to explain away

<hr>

[28] Bultmann, *Offenbarung und Heilsgeschehen*, p. 66f.
[29] Bultmann, *Theologie des Neuen Testaments*, Tübingen 1948, p. 300.

this clear significance of the passage.[30] Bultmann rightly refuses to let this pass, but now Paul is criticised for his "fatal argument" in 1 Cor. xv. 3ff.[31] "The argument in this passage is fatal, because it seeks to give a proof of the credibility of the *Kerygma*."[32] In fact Paul's line of argument is in flat contradiction with Bultmann's thesis. Nor does Paul in other passages renounce legitimation. In the introduction to his epistles he presents himself to the churches—and so he will have done also in his missionary preaching which led to the foundation of the churches—as a man called and sent by Jesus Christ, as a messenger with authority who was called in a concrete historical event. Thus he decisively refers behind the *kerygma* to the historical data, that he is a witness to the appearing of the risen Lord, and an ambassador commissioned by Him.

If this holds good in Paul's case biblically and theologically, the question of historical fact is essential in all Christian preaching, and refuses to be silenced. Bultmann formulates his position thus: "The word of preaching meets us as God's word, in relation to which we can raise no questions of legitimation. Rather does it ask us whether we are willing to believe or not." That sounds very illuminating; of course one cannot raise questions of legitimation when confronted by what bears witness to itself as the word of God, one can only believe or disbelieve. But the formula "word of God" is here too simple, and conceals the real problem. The problem is this; preaching has a double content in inseparable unity; it is a report of things that have happened, happened in our human history at a determinate place and time. And secondly it is, in the indicative and imperative, a witness of the significance of this event for salvation and judgment.

[30] Barth, *Die Auferstehung der Toten*, Munich 1926, pp. 75ff.
[31] Bultmann, *Offenbarung und Heilsgeschehen*, p. 64.
[32] Bultmann, *Kerygma und Mythos*, Hamburg 1948, VOL. I, p. 144.

The *kerygma* of the apostles and of the Church has always also historical content, it is always in addition witness to historical facts. It is different in the case of the word of God proclaimed by the prophets. Here the moment of witness to historical event is missing. The question of legitimation is a different one in the case of the apostles from that in the case of the prophets, precisely because of the relation to past history

H. Strathmann says on the concept of "witness" in Luke: "The peculiarity of the object with which this witness deals [the facts of the history of Jesus, especially the facts of His Resurrection], has the consequence that in the concept of 'the witness' two things are indissolubly bound up with each other, the narration of certain facts, and the preaching of their significance, a preaching which springs from faith, confesses faith, and appeals for faith. Witness to facts and witness to the truth coincide—the inevitable consequence of the fact that in the gospel we have to do with a historical revelation . . . . We are not dealing with any doctrines or myths or speculations, but with facts, which happened at a definite place, at a definite time, in the clear light of history, which can be determined and on which we can rely. And for this reason the names of witnesses must be given. . . ."[33]

H. Diem says rightly; "There should be general agreement about the fact that the New Testament authors are in the highest degree concerned about the actual happening of the history of Jesus which they proclaim."[34] I find it, accordingly, all the more difficult to understand Diem, when he can yet say on the next page, that one way of missing the significance of Christ through unbelief "would be the attempt to withdraw from the impact of the preaching of [this story] and thus to place oneself in a

[33] In *Theologisches Wörterbuch zum Neuen Testament*, ed. G. Kittel, henceforth cited as Kittel, VOL. IV, Stuttgart 1933, pp. 495ff.

[34] *Dogmatik*, p. 113, Eng. trans., p. 125.

position of detachment from it, by seeking to base its reality on purely historical grounds."[35] Diem quotes with approval the exposition of the concept of "witness" already cited, and other sentences about Luke; but I must now ask him whether Luke himself does not come under his strictures, since unquestionably Luke seeks "to base its reality on purely historical grounds" (see the prologue to his gospel 1.1-4). Diem—and this is perhaps the solution of the problem facing me here—clearly distinguishes between two things. First, there is the *interest* in the fact that the history of Christ which we preach actually happened (this he finds in the New Testament, and this is, in his judgment, theologically necessary and legitimate). And second, there is "the *independent* interest in the historical truth of what is reported."[36] The existence of the latter in the New Testament is denied, and is described as a failure through unbelief to reach the significance of the history of Jesus, and thus declared to be theologically illegitimate. But what does "independent interest" mean? Faith, it is true, has an interest here only because the factuality of the matters reported is a part of the authority of the preaching; faith's interest is thus not in a "historical fact as such, apart from its proclamation."[37] But although the interest *in this sense* is not "independent," yet the question as to the factuality as such is independent within the context of the encounter with the preaching, and must also receive its independent answer, just as Luke answers it "in his strong interest in exposing clearly the historical foundations of the evangelical message,"[38] and that clearly by historical means, i.e. the naming of witnesses and citation of sources (Lk. 1.1ff.). Luke in fact makes the "claim to be heard as a reliable historian and to be

[35] *Dogmatik*, p. 114, Eng. trans., p. 126
[36] *Op. cit.*, p. 109, Eng. trans., p. 120.
[37] *Op. cit.*, p. 111, Eng. trans., p. 122.
[38] Strathmann in Kittel, VOL. IV, pp. 495ff.

received with trust."[39] His intention is in his own fashion
to prove on historical principles and by historical means
the trustworthiness of the gospel history. Is this theologically illegitimate? E. Käsemann, finds the way in
which Luke develops the interest in history "dangerous."[40]

The question is: In the case of the apostolic and Church
kerygma, which is witness to a historical revelation, is it not
a part of the authority of the preaching as word of God,
that it can claim to have its source in genuine history?
To repeat our thesis once more, the formula used by
Bultmann—"word of God"—conceals the problem which
is set for us by the double character of the apostolic
witness both as a report of determinate facts and as
preaching which appeals for a decision. The case is
different with the word of the prophets of the Old Testament. There Bultmann's principle does apply. But it
cannot be simply applied to the preaching of the apostles
and the Church, because we have here to deal with the
witness to things that happened in history. Here preaching, in view of its historic content enclosed in the *kerygma*,
requires "legitimation," and here the question of that
legitimation must be raised. Bultmann's principle holds
for what we may call in the narrower sense the kerygmatic
content of preaching, for the confession of the saving
significance of what has happened, a confession which
appeals for decision, and calls on men to acknowledge
that significance. If preaching says to me: "The death
and resurrection of Christ concern you in your existence,
He died for your sin, and was raised for your justification:
acknowledge that fact, and let yourself be reconciled in
Christ to God," then in fact in this case I can only say
"Yes" or "No." Here I must believe; to question here the
right of such preaching, i.e. its right to relate what has

[39] K. H. Rengstorf in *Das Neue Testament Deutsch*, VOL. III, 8th edn.
Göttingen 1958, on LK. 1.3.
[40] *Z. Th. K.*, LI (1954), pp. 137, 141.

happened to my existence, is already a decision of unbelief.

Here there is no legitimation except that which is constituted by the message itself. Here my conscience is touched, and I sin if I begin to ask for legitimation instead of knowing that I am touched and questioned. But it is different when we consider the historical content of the message. If I say "Yes" or "No" to the question whether the events of Good Friday and Easter touch *me*, then in every case I presuppose, consciously or unconsciously, that the event of which the message speaks is a real, consequently also an historical, event. Thus I presuppose that the messengers of Jesus Christ, who call me to decision, have trustworthy knowledge about this Jesus and can impart it to me; that "Jesus Christ" is consequently not the name of a mythical figure, that the accounts in the gospel which purport to tell of Him are not the deceptive projection of a myth into history; that He really was crucified because of His preaching and His claim to authority, and that the report of His showing Himself as risen from the dead is credibly attested. This side of the matter—that is the question of the historicity of the historical content of the message—short-circuits Bultmann's talk about the illegitimacy of the question of legitimation. Here legitimation *is* necessary. It does not need to be said that this legitimation of a historical kind cannot prove the character of the preaching *as word of God*, nor does it claim to do so. This character, and that means God's action as such in past events of history, cannot be proved. It is known only in faith. The theologians who veto any retrospective inquiry as to the historical foundations of the *kerygma*, are clearly anxious lest it should become an attempt to find an historical proof of the character of the history of Jesus as revelation and act of God, as if here historical knowledge were seeking to supplant faith. But none of us who here oppose Bultmann, is making any such suggestion. None of us wishes to refurbish the doctrine that the supernatural appeared manifest on the plane of history.[41] The revelatory character of the history of Jesus is not known by means of historical reflexion or historical reasoning. But on the other hand, it is not known *without these*. For the gospel deals with facts which, it is claimed, happened in this history of ours; it has "historical facts" as content, and its foundation in history is a part of its credibility.[42]

The veto on the attempt to ask the retrospective question behind the *kerygma* means that the "historical Jesus" is theologically of no importance to us. To describe Bultmann's position in E. Käsemann's terms; "Christian faith is here understood as faith in the exalted Lord, for which the historical Jesus has no longer constitutive significance."[43] "Thus we are forbidden to go behind the *kerygma*, using it as a source to reconstruct a historical Jesus. That would be precisely the Χριστὸς κατὰ σάρκα who belongs to the past. Not the historical Jesus, but Jesus Christ who is preached, is the Lord."[44] The "historical Jesus" and "Jesus Christ who is preached" are thus severed from each other and opposed to each other with a "not . . . but." What is valid in this disjunction (it is the element common to Bultmann and Kähler) does not need to be mentioned again. But what remains of the identity of the earthly Jesus and the Jesus Christ who is preached? Bultmann does not of course deny it, but it is theologically of importance to him only in so far as the risen Christ (in Bultmann's sense) and the preached

[41] Cf. here my *Grundriss der Dogmatik*, Erlangen 1929, VOL. I, § 11; and *Die Christliche Wahrheit*, p. 41.

[42] Cf. Künneth's criticism of Bultmann's conception of revelation (in Ellwein, Kinder, and Künneth, *Zur Entmythologisierung*, pp. 78ff.): "Revelation gives to history the form of 'a sign' and includes it in the salvation event. . . . From this it follows that here we have also to reckon with an historical knowledge of the historical deposits of revelation. This *notitia* is accessible even to unbelief. But authentic knowledge of such events as the revelation of God is accessible to faith alone."

[43] *Z. Th. K.*, LI (1954), p. 126.

[44] Bultmann, *Glauben und Verstehen*, Tübingen 1933, VOL. I, p. 208.

Christ is the crucified one, that is, the real man, Jesus of Nazareth. On the other hand the picture of His person is obviously theologically without interest. He is indeed also unrecognisable because He is overlaid by the *kerygma*. And apart from this, an interest in the personal picture of Jesus would be a "knowing Christ after the flesh" which, according to Paul (II Cor. v.16), is done away for the believer.[45] It would be an understanding according to the flesh, a mere reckoning with objects in the empirical world.[46] "The Χριστὸς κατὰ σάρκα is no concern of ours": we can look on calmly at the bonfire which radical criticism like that of Bultmann in his *Geschichte der Synoptischen Tradition* has made. "I calmly let it burn, for I see that what is burnt here is all the fantasy pictures of the 'Life of Jesus' theology, and that this is the Χριστὸς κατὰ σάρκα Himself."[47] Thus not only the nineteenth-century "Lives of Jesus" are consigned to the flames—here again Bultmann is at one with Kähler—but also the picture of the earthly Christ Himself. We have seen how different was Kähler's opinion on this point. The passage from II Cor. v.16 ("We know Christ no more after the flesh") is here misused. The words κατὰ σάρκα do not go with the object "Christ," but with the verb "know." This Bultmann himself holds "more probable,"[48] but adds; "The decision is of no significance for the meaning in the general context, for a Christ known κατὰ σάρκα is a Χριστὸς κατὰ σάρκα." And that means, on Bultmann's interpretation, "Christ in respect of His being an object in the empirical world. . . . The Christ who is an object in the empirical world is perceived in the manner that objects in the world are seen." This then would in fact be the historical Jesus, who is known in a historical manner. But does Paul say

---

[45] *Glauben und Verstehen*, pp. 206ff.   [46] *Op. cit.*, p. 207.
[47] Bultmann, "Zur Frage der Christologie," in *Zwischen den Zeiten*, Munich 1927, p. 56f., reprinted in *Glauben und Verstehen*, VOL. I, p. 100f.
[48] *Theologie des Neuen Testaments*, p. 234.

35

this, and is it theologically legitimate to belittle and deny the interest of faith in the historical Jesus? Paul means something quite different. "We know Christ now only in faith in Him, and now no more by the mind of the flesh as I dealt with Him hitherto when I hated and persecuted Him in His Church, because I was under the bondage of the law." There is absolutely no reference in II Cor. v.16 to a Χριστὸς κατὰ σάρκα, and the whole phrase has nothing to do with "an object in the empirical world." The antithesis is not between perceiving Jesus as an object in the empirical world and acknowledging Him in faith as Lord, but between despising and persecuting Him, because one is bound under slavery to the Jewish Law, and acknowledging Him in faith as Lord. As the modern interpretation is un-Pauline, so it must also be theologically repudiated. Luther says that Christ is indeed known *in carne*, but not *secundum carnem*.[49] Faith has a burning interest in the character of Jesus's actions among men, for here it seeks and finds God's presence "in the flesh." We understand well why Bultmann and others ban from theology the "evaluation" of the "personality of Jesus."[50] That was a necessary antithesis to the "reverence for Jesus" of the liberal theology. But in so doing more is surrendered than faith can afford to lose. I must here repeat what I wrote in 1929 in a review of E. Brunner's *Der Mittler*; "I believe that in the next years we shall have remorsefully to readmit much into Christology that it is fashionable now to despise under the title of 'the personality of Christ'."[51] How thoroughly Luther steeped himself in the concrete character of the converse of Jesus with men, in order to grasp therein the ways of God's dealings with us! And is this to be forbidden to us on theological

[49] Luther, *Werke*, Weimar edn. (*Kritische Gesamtausgabe*, ed. J. C. F. Knaake, 1883), VOL. XXIII, p. 734.

[50] Bultmann, *Glauben und Verstehen*, VOL. I, pp. 206ff.

[51] *Theologische Literaturzeitung*, henceforth cited as *Th. Lz.*, 1929, p. 476f., reprinted in Althaus, *Theologische Aufsätze*, Gütersloh 1935, VOL. II, p. 178.

grounds? In dealing with the details of the converse of Jesus with men, everything for faith depends on the fact that they are not an ideal picture portrayed in a sacred legend of the *kerygma*, but a clear historical reality. We emphasise: faith is interested in the character of Jesus's actions, not in His "inner life," however certain it may be that a light is thrown on the latter by His actions. But we mean the character of Jesus's actions even when we are inquiring about the person of Jesus—even when we ask about His character, for by this we mean the character of His *actions*. Thus we are not concerned with "a personality existing independently of His work, with certain concerns, inclinations and feelings peculiar to itself."[52]

[52] As Barth rightly says in *Kirchliche Dogmatik*, VOL. III, PT II, Zollikon-Zürich 1948, p. 67. Cf. also my review of Bultmann's *Der Begriff der Offenbarung im Neuen Testament* in *Th. Lz.*, 1929, pp. 413ff., esp. p. 415f.

In criticism of *Kerygma* theology the following names should also be cited. Ellwein: "The *Kerygma* becomes a hypostasis suspended in an empty void" (*Zur Entmythologisierung*, p. 31); E. Steinbach: "The *Kerygma*, according to this strange theory, is left hanging absolutely in the air; after all other miracles have been dispensed with, it becomes itself the solitary miracle. Bultmann's Kerygmatic Christ is a spectre compared with the historical reality (in *Mythos und Geschichte*, Tübingen 1951, pp. 14ff., esp. p. 20).

Translator's note: About 500 words more of this note have, with Dr Althaus's permission, been omitted from the English translation. The reason for this abbreviation is that the omitted paragraphs serve rather to indicate that distinguished contemporary German theologians agree with the above criticisms, than to add anything fresh to the argument itself.

3

The Concept of History and the Historical

THESE clear issues are today being obscured by the concept of history and the historical which are put forward in defence of Bultmann's position. Here we have to deal principally with Friedrich Gogarten. In his book *Entmythologisierung und Kirche* he brings this particular concept to the defence of Bultmann.[1]

According to Gogarten only those past events can be called historic which disclose to me a possibility of my own existence, and, by so doing, challenge me by the claim of their authority to make a historic decision. The following sentences may serve to define Gogarten's concept of history. "Wherever we have to do with history we have to do with the historic character of human existence."[2] The historic character of human existence means that man knows himself to be responsible for the form of the world.[3] "I see the constitutive element of history (*Geschichte*) and that which makes human existence and the world historic, in the responsibility of man for the world."[4] According to Gogarten it is only in the Christian faith that the historic character of man and the world has been disclosed. All this can be comprehensively expressed as follows; history consists of those events which stand in relation to the historic character of human existence in the above sense;

---

[1] F. Gogarten, *Entmythologisierung und Kirche*, 2nd edn. Stuttgart 1954. See also E. Kinder, *Das neuzeitliche Geschichtsdenken und die Theologie. Antwort an Fr. Gogarten.* Luthertum, Heft XII, Berlin 1954.

[2] Gogarten, *Entmythologisierung und Kirche*, p. 45.

[3] *Op. cit.*, p. 54.   [4] *Op. cit.*, p. 10.

i.e. events which constitute a challenge to responsible man.

This conception of the historic is objectionable on two grounds: Firstly, it departs completely from the concept of history and the historic current in scholarly usage. It is the product of caprice, and makes it hard to come to an understanding with the historian who investigates past history.

It must be acknowledged that the relationship to man is an essential ingredient in the concept of history and the historic. Where man appears as an agent, we speak of history, in contradistinction from nature. We experience history when actions performed by men impinge upon us and influence us in our common life. Today it has become customary in theology to limit the concept of history more narrowly, and to speak of history in the strict sense of the word only where the past at the same time is present for us, is contemporary with us, and calls us to responsibility and decision. History and the historic should then be distinguished from mere facts which might be described as "the historical" (*das Historische*), "with which we can obviously concern ourselves without touching the realm of the historic (*geschichtlich*) at all".[5] Then one can say: "the historical is history (*Geschichte*) in a state of petrifaction. Its historic significance is not at all brought to light by mere statement and tradition."[6] The past as such, which does not prove itself to be an event which calls me to responsibility and decision and thus becomes my contemporary, is excluded from the concept of the historic. This existentialist concept of history and the historic is found today among theologians and philosophers. But for the historians who still regard their discipline as the science of history, as an investigation into history, it is wholly unsuitable. They cannot refrain from calling past events, as such, history (*Geschichte*). This too is indeed

[5] E. Steinbach in *Mythos und Geschichte*, p. 9.
[6] Käsemann in *Z. Th. K.*, LI (1954), p. 132.

contemporary with us in so far as it has more or less contributed to make our historical situation what it is; i.e.
by causal means. Thus far it is present with us today.
But, in the first place, that is by no means true of all events
in the past which are the object of historical study. And
secondly, and more important, this presence with us of
the past, in so far as it has contributed to produce the
situation in which we live today, is quite different from
the presence to which the existentialist conception of
history and the historic refers.[7] But whatever be our
decision upon this issue, whether it be advisable that
theology and philosophy set up one concept of their own
of the historic (*das Geschichtliche*) which is much narrower
than the concept of the historic (*das Geschichtliche*) current
in the science of history and in the philosophy of history
in the past, in every case the historical-factual element
is a part of that concept. True, the "historic" is distinct
from the merely factual, and means more than mere fact,
but it does include the notion of historical fact, and *does
not exist* without it. Let the past have the power to make
itself present to the existence of men today, it is for all that
also past. The historical is not the same thing as the
historic in the modern sense of the latter concept, but the
historic is never without the historical, it is also historical,
and as such it is the object of historical inquiry and knowledge.

Secondly, the new concept as used by Bultmann and
Gogarten serves to neutralise the historical-factual element
inasmuch as in the case of the *kerygma* the question of
historical fact is declared illegitimate. We must show this
by giving some quotations from Gogarten. He declares
"that the authentic history and the historic character
(*Geschichte, Geschichtlichkeit*) of the events to which the New
Testament bears witness, is not to be sought in their
objective historically ascertainable character as facts that

[7] Cf. Althaus, *Christliche Wahrheit*, § 14.

40

actually happened, but in the *kerygma*, the witness of preaching to the gracious approach which God made in this history to men and to the world."[8] And: "The *kerygma* does not set out to be, or at least does not in the first place set out to be, anything like an account of past happenings. ... That would be true, even if something which has happened had been announced in the message of the herald. This event would then be of such a kind as to challenge the person to whom the message of the herald is addressed."[9] We note in the last passage the qualification of the "not," by the following "not in the first place." What is true in these sentences, and what no one denies, is that the believer is not just concerned with events in general, but with such events as become God's word to him, concern him, and are intended for him. But faith is really interested in the objective fact of their having happened, in the sense of historical factuality, and has been—as the New Testament shows—from the earliest days of Christianity until today.

The history wherein God deals with men is essentially a history which genuinely happened. It is senseless to separate the two elements of the events to which the apostolic preaching bears witness in this way; on the one hand its character as an actual fact of history and on the other its character as bearer of God's action, so that one is emphasised more than the other, given preference to the other, and termed "authentic."[10] For both are a unity, and in this unity both elements are equally "authentic." The salvation event takes place in happenings to whose historicity (in the hitherto usual sense of the word) witness is borne, and without which the salvation event is not present.

It is strange how Gogarten rejects as theologically

<hr/>

[8] Gogarten, *Entmythologisierung und Kirche*, p. 44f.   [9] *Op. cit.*, p. 69.
[10] See Gogarten: "the authentic history . . . not, or not in the first place, something in the nature of a report" (*op. cit.*, p. 69).

illegitimate this interest of faith, as the critics of Bultmann have represented it in their writings against him. The interest in objective history arises, he tells us, from an outmoded metaphysical way of thinking, which has been transcended by the new historic approach.[11] We are told that it is based on an out of date subject-object-thinking, from which modern philosophy has set us free. It is thus, we are told, theologically reactionary. But why such far-fetched explanations, why all this philosophical carping at "objective historicity" and the so-called subject-object mode of thinking? The Lutheran theologians, with whom Gogarten disputes so ungraciously, are anything but the victims of an effete philosophy and theory of knowledge. Their criticism is based on the New Testament; they perceive that in it there is no *kerygma* standing in the void, but that it refers back to events, which are reported as such. What has interest in the reliability of the narratives, in the fact that the history of Jesus really happened, got to do with metaphysical thinking, with a subject-object mode of thinking? It seems to me that this great display of historical-philosophical and epistemological considerations obscures the simplicity of the question which is here in dispute.[12]

[11] Gogarten, *Entmythologisierung und Kirche*, p. 52.
[12] Diem (*Dogmatik*, p. 64) speaks of Bultmann's "evasion of the question of historical fact." There are for Bultmann "no historical events in whose real happening he could or should be interested" (p. 63, Eng. trans., p. 67). Diem is right in indicating that the previously mentioned concept of the "historic" leads to the result that the text of, say, the Easter narratives, is no longer interrogated with reference to the event it proclaims, "but a certain idea of what constitutes history is applied to it as a criterion" (p. 82, Eng. trans., pp. 89-90). The interest of the exegete, and consequently of exegesis itself, lies within the limits of his concept of history and historicity (*Geschichte und Geschichtlichkeit*).

4

Bultmann's Inconsistency

THE veto on questions about the historical basis of the *kerygma* is particularly hard to understand when it comes from a man like Rudolf Bultmann, who is a historian, and has written a book about Jesus. We must ask whether there is not a wide gulf between Bultmann the historian of the book on Jesus, and the systematic theologian of the *kerygma* theology. What, in his opinion, is the relation between the work of historical criticism which he has achieved in his *Geschichte der Synoptischen Tradition* and in his *Jesus*, and *kerygma* theology? Has the former only a negative significance for the latter, or is there a positive significance also? Hermann Diem concludes that historical study has no positive significance for faith in the thought of Bultmann.[1] Bultmann "tries persistently to get behind the *kerygma* of the texts [in the gospels] by critical methods, in order to establish what in fact happened, and he does so with the same resources (although sharpened by the methods of form-criticism) as the whole of historical-critical research before him. But he does not do so—and here is the decisive difference —in order to base faith on the historical conclusions attained, but, on the contrary, in order to make impossible any such basis for faith, and thus he has greater scope for the most radical results than any of his predecessors. Always, for him, faith must be made insecure and all historical foundations withdrawn from it. That historical

[1] Diem, *Dogmatik*, p. 83, Eng. trans., p. 90.

criticism (at any rate in regard to the history of Jesus) might have another, positive, significance is not apparent." Strangely enough this "shaking the security of faith" is supposed to fit in with the Reformers' theology of *sola fide*, and to vindicate this theology on the question of faith in Jesus Christ. Emmanuel Hirsch had expressed a similar opinion in his book *Die Auferstehungsgeschichten und der Christliche Glaube*.[2]

We shall return to this misuse of Luther's theology. It seems in fact that, in Bultmann's opinion, there is no positive relation between his historical work and his *kerygma* theology. We must indeed speak with H. Diem of "inconsistency" in Bultmann.[3] Bultmann himself says: "My book on Jesus is not *kerygma*, nor does the historical Jesus meet us in the *kerygma*; what meets us in the *kerygma* is Jesus as the Christ, as eschatological phenomenon. Neither Paul nor John bring us into historical contact with the historical Jesus.[4] The synoptic writers do so only when they are read with the intention of asking what, historically, lies behind the *kerygma*. But when read as they meant their work to be read, they do not. But in order for Jesus to be understood as an eschatological phenomenon (i.e. as the Saviour through whom God frees man from the world, by judging the world and giving the future to the believer), all that is necessary is that the fact of His having come should be proclaimed, as happens with the utmost clearness in John."[5] This last sentence is characteristic of Bultmann's Christology. It is Johannine in so far as in John's Gospel in fact the actual

[2] Tübingen 1940. See also my criticism of Hirsch in *Die Wahrheit des Kirchlichen Osterglaubens*, Gütersloh 1941, pp. 59ff.

[3] Diem, *Dogmatik*, pp. 84-7, Eng. trans., pp. 91-5.

[4] *Translator's note*: Here is one of Bultmann's inconsistencies in the use of his chosen terms, mentioned above. The word used is "geschichtlich," which ought to be translated "historic"; but the logic of the passage demands "historical", which has accordingly been used.

[5] Bultmann, *Kerygma und Mythos*, VOL. I, p. 149.

44

features of the Lord, as the synoptic writers show Him to us, are withdrawn from us, and the ever-repeated assertion of the *coming* of the Son and His significance is thrust before us. So the witness borne by John is abstract compared with the synoptic witness. The same is true of Bultmann's *kerygma* Christology.

He does indeed declare: "I do not deny the close relationship of the Easter *kerygma* to the earthly and crucified Jesus."[6] But this remains for him an absolutely general and abstract statement, which receives no concrete expression whatsoever in the *kerygma* theology. There is no concrete continuity in Bultmann's theology between the historical Jesus who was the subject of his historical work, and the apostolic preaching. Various writers have made this criticism of Bultmann. Eduard Ellwein declares that in Bultmann "the bridge between the historical Jesus and the preached Christ has, so to speak, collapsed."[7] Does the *person* of Jesus with its concrete characteristics play any part in the *kerygma* theology? Günther Bornkamm declares: "Jesus has become a mere fact of salvation and is no longer a person."[8] The fact that the person of Jesus as such (of whose concrete characteristics we can, in Bultmann's words "now know practically nothing")[9] has no place in the *kerygma*, leads to serious theological consequences. The power of the Gospel to overcome our unbelief depends on the fact that the *kerygma* includes the gospels with their concrete picture of Jesus. In the picture of the man Jesus we lay hold of the character of God, in the spiritual countenance of Jesus we behold the countenance of God. The living eyes of a man look at us out of the gospels, and compel our faith. The *kerygma* is a statement, a dogma, if we do not see it filled out by the

[6] *Op. cit.*, p. 144. [7] In *Zur Entmythologisierung*, p. 23.
[8] G. Bornkamm, "Mythos und Evangelium," in *Theologische Existenz heute*, n.s. XXVI (1951), p. 18.
[9] Bultmann, *Jesus*, Berlin 1926, p. 12.

living picture of Jesus as the gospels portray Him. Without this, how can the *kerygma* compel us to believe? If, as Bultmann says, it places before us the question of decision, then, sundered from the picture of Jesus, it meets us as *law*. I am confronted with a decision, I am questioned, I must answer; but of the power that can compel me to believe, there is not a word. And how can the *kerygma*, emptied of the historical personality of Jesus, have this power? Thus the Gospel meets me only as law, as a demand for belief. But the New Testament tells us that the Word became flesh, a human personal life, in whose features we should seek the features of the Father (Jn. xiv.9). In the *kerygma* theology the Word has become—*kerygma*! *Kerygma* Christology has no need of the actual features of the earthly Jesus. . . .[10]

[10] *Translator's note*: At this point there follows in the German text a note in small print containing about 200 words, which, with Dr Althaus's permission, has been omitted from the English version, and for the same reason as the omission in Ch. 2, n. 52.

5

Word of God and Faith

IN defence of its veto on the question of the historical
legitimation of the Gospel, *kerygma* theology appeals also
to Luther, and claims, in contrast with its "ecclesiastical"
critics, to take seriously Luther's view of the word of God
and faith. Let us examine closely Gogarten's attempt
thus to claim Luther's support. In contrast with the
interest in "objective salvation events," Gogarten points
to the "word-character" of revelation, which, we are told,
excludes any interest in the facts lying behind the word.
"The reality on which at least Luther's faith lives, and is
nourished, is the reality of the word, and that reality
alone. . . . The reality which discloses itself to faith is the
reality of the word. Thus in so far as an event has the
character of a word and is understood in this word-
character, the believer grasps in it the reality which is
vital to him."[1] "The reality with which faith is concerned,
is never a different type of reality than that which belongs
to the word, and in no case can it be called an 'objective'
'factual' reality." Bultmann's theological work, if anyone's—so Gogarten believes—can help Church theology
"so to think and speak of the reality of the revelation, that
it is understood as the New Testament and the Reformers
understood it, that is, as a 'word-reality,' as *the* reality
which is proper to God's word, and not any other kind of
reality."[2] "The genus of the reality of revelation" is that

[1] Gogarten, *Entmythologisierung und Kirche*, p. 104.
[2] *Op. cit.*, p. 111.

47

of the divine word. God's revelation is, indeed, act, "but the act happens through the word and in the word."[3] "God's act and acts have the character proper to, and appertaining to, the word." If we take this seriously, then we can no longer attempt, as Gogarten says that W. Künneth and E. Kinder do, "to underpin the reality of revelation."

Gogarten and the rest of us hold the same view of the New Testament conception, and the Reformer's conception of revelation; there is no conflict between us on this point. But I am bound to think that he has drawn illegitimate conclusions from this premiss. Without doubt God's revelation reaches us in the word, and in no other way; in the word of preaching the salvation events become real for us and "find" us. On this we are agreed. But the word of preaching is not only a word that addresses us. As well as being a message of salvation it is at the same time a report about a historical event which happened. Thus it refers back to an event, a reality, which is not identical with it, but to which it is retrospectively related. For it is witness to something, and this "something" is also a historic fact. In view of this we cannot equate the word and the reality of the revelation as Gogarten does. Rather is the word the salvation event in so far as it refers us to an event which took place for our salvation, because it speaks of facts in history. The "word of God" has in it elements of human historical witness. Gogarten's criticism of Kinder: "The word itself, however, on Kinder's view is not the salvation event, it only speaks of that event,"[4] represents a theologically impossible antithesis, for Kinder and the rest of us say rather: "The word is the salvation event, because it speaks of the salvation event." Thus we must affirm strictly as the simple truth what Gogarten chalks up against his opponents as a

[3] Gogarten, *Entmythologisierung und Kirche*, p. 100.
[4] *Op. cit.*, p. 103.

failure to understand the true sense of the gospel; the gospel is "act bearing word-character" *precisely because* it is "information about something which this word does not immediately contain, and which does not immediately happen in the word, precisely because it is information about a fact."[5] (Observe here again in Gogarten the quite impossible disjunction by means of a "not . . . but" of things that stand in inseparable conjunction. Gogarten opposes to one another "act bearing word-character" and "report about a fact"—while in reality he ought to say "Act bearing word-character *because* report about a fact.") After all the word did not just become flesh in the *kerygma*, was not incarnate in it, but in the historical Jesus Christ! The "word-character" of the revelation, the act-character of the word of preaching must not be used to neutralise and explain away the fact that the word stands in relationship of witness to an event other than itself. And what has our objection to this got to do with metaphysical thinking, or with entanglement in an out-of-date subject-object mode of thinking? Surely it comes rather from simple reflexion on the New Testament reality of the message.

In Gogarten's doctrine of the word of God, at least as he expounds it in his book *Entmythologisierung und Kirche*, the historical element is wholly missing. Yet without this the authority of the Bible cannot be understood. "True, this word is attested by the Bible, but that is not why it creates faith, but because it is the promise of God, the *promissio Dei*. The word does not gain its validity from its attestation by the Bible, but the other way round. The Bible gains its authority from bearing witness to this word." The Bible has great authority, because it bears witness to the word on which faith relies. "But certainly it is not this authority of the Bible by which faith lives. No, rather, our faith depends upon no other authority than

[5] *Entmythologisierung und Kirche*, p. 102.

that of the word of God itself. The word, just because it is
the word of God, has its authority in itself."[6] These
sentences of Gogarten seem to be nothing but a clear
reproduction of Luther's teaching on the word of God.
But that is not the case. They simplify matters too much,
and do not let it appear that there is also a historical
element which belongs to the word of God which is
uttered in the message, and to which the Bible bears
witness. The historical element consists in this, that here
trustworthy witnesses speak of a history that happened in
definite historical places. We must not overlook—as so
oftens happens when appeal is made to Luther's doctrine
of the word of God—that Luther, in his doctrine of holy
scripture as the word of God, always presupposed, usually
tacitly, the credibility of the book as a whole as the product
of the Holy Spirit. In fact, Luther believed in what
Gogarten calls "the metaphysical quality of a book which
came miraculously into being."[7] It is unnecessary to say
that this theory is no longer tenable. But—and this is
usually forgotten today—a decisive truth which found
expression in this theory, still holds good and is indispensable for our doctrine of the word of God and holy scripture. That is, that it is not enough to say that because the
word is the word of God, it has its authority in itself. This
by no means fully expresses the specific authority of the
apostolic preaching. In addition to the distinguishing
mark of its particular content—to use Luther's expression, "it deals with Christ"—it has this other characteristic, that in it we have to deal with the "first witnesses,"
with a witness given in historical proximity and immediate relationship to the history of Jesus.[8] The general
concept of the word of God does not underline this special
content. So it is not enough to say, in relation to the

[6] *Entmythologisierung und Kirche,* pp. 25ff.
[7] *Op. cit.,* p. 26.
[8] See my *Christliche Wahrheit,* § 18.1.

apostolic *kerygma*: "The word, just because it is the word of God, has its authority in itself." For this statement does not do justice to the historical element in the authority. Nor may this historical element be overlooked even in the contemporary preaching of the Church; its authority depends on the fact that the present word of preaching is interpretation of the apostolic witness, whose authority depends on its "authenticity"—that is, on the historical reference, that it goes back to the witnesses of the history of Jesus, including the Resurrection. Gogarten's antithesis "The word is not valid because the Bible testifies to it, but the other way round; the Bible has its authority because it testifies to this word," is wrong in so far as an essential element of the authority of the apostolic "word of God" (cf. 1 Thess. 11.13) is, that it is proved to be "authentic" by its inclusion in the canon of the New Testament scriptures in which the documents of the apostolic age are collected. And so the sentence rejected by Gogarten is theologically right, despite him. Admittedly it does not say all that has to be said about authority, but only gives us a side of the truth which cannot be dismissed as of no importance. It is justified in that the validity of the word depends on the fact that "the Bible testifies to it"—in the sense that it does not come from the third or fourth century after Christ, but from the apostolic age. It is strange and inconceivable that the *kerygma* theology wholly, as it seems, misses this side of the matter. Has then the whole historical enterprise of introductions to the New Testament and history of the Canon no theological, no dogmatic significance? Is theology meddling in other people's concerns, or is it doing necessary work when it undertakes to investigate and to prove the authenticity of the New Testament writings, and their origin in the times of primitive Christianity, from the hands of the apostles or the pupils of the apostles, that is, their origin in the genuine tradition? Is it a theological

51

undertaking or not, to pose the question of historical originality or authenticity? There can be no doubt that Bultmann and Gogarten consider these endeavours of introductions to the New Testament necessary and indispensable. But if so, they must concede that the question as to the authority of the *kerygma* is disastrously simplified if it is thought that everything necessary has been said when the thesis "the word has its authority in itself" has been enunciated—unless the factor of genuine tradition is tacitly included in the phrase "in itself." A doctrine of "the word of God" in the New Testament sense is inadequate if the historical factor of tradition in the doctrine is suppressed. The authority of the word of God is not indeed established for us any longer by a metaphysical miraculous character possessed by the Bible, but it is in part established by the historical element of the original tradition, of authenticity. This element does not authenticate itself to faith "in a vacuum." It must be established by historical investigation.[9] Here, then, the Reformers' affirmation of the self-authenticating word of God is not sufficient. It was no falling away from Luther, when old Lutheran dogmatic theology was not satisfied merely to speak with the Calvinists of the witness of the Holy Spirit, which gives us the certainty that Scripture is the word of God, but at the same time declared that the historical questions concerning the origin of a book, concerning its authenticity, are not to be decided by the witness of the Holy Spirit, but by the witness of the earliest Church; and itself investigated the canonicity of the separate books, with such historical arguments as lay within the reach of contemporary scholarships. If theology, in the name of the Reformers' doctrine of the word of God and of faith, were to neglect the historical question of the authenticity of the apostolic preaching, and thus no longer to ask for the credentials of the message,

[9] Cf. my *Christliche Wahrheit*, § 17.3.

it would be rejecting the true humanity and the *kenosis* of Christ. For the latter means that God's word has submitted itself wholly to the law of historical time, and comes to us in the very human form of tradition, of historical witness passed on from mouth to mouth, and thus, as tradition, must submit to the question of legitimacy, in the sense of authenticity.

But this question cannot be silenced when we confront the apostolic *kerygma*. Just as in the introductions to the New Testament, in the history of the canon and of the primitive Church, theology must seek for assurance that the New Testament, and with it the *kerygma*, comes from the apostles, so it cannot forgo the question as to whether the apostolic *kerygma* has its origin in the events of real history.

The statement: "the word, because it is the word of God, has its authority in itself," is true without qualification of God's *Law*, but not of the *Gospel*. For in the proclamation of the Law there is no historical reference of the witness to a concrete event, an element which belongs to the Gospel.

The word, in so far as it is a proclamation of the claim of God's will on man, has indeed its authority in itself. Of itself it convinces me, and binds my conscience. It attests itself by itself as the eternal will of God, for which I am created. But God's act, of which the Gospel speaks, is contingent event. To it there corresponds the concept of the witness, and moreover both in the contingent sense and in the unique sense of that term, since he is a "witness to the truth" and at the same time a "witness to fact."[10] In a double sense he is an original witness, thus, in the sense of historical originality, a witness at first hand. The Law needs no witness in the historical sense, but the Gospel does.

Further, the assertion, by means of which a virtue is

[10] See above, pp., 29-30.

53

made out of the historical uncertainty of the history of Jesus—that faith, as the Reformers understood it, is truly itself only when all historical supports are removed from it, when it has no longer any "earthly" foundation—can only be described as a theological error. This is true both of the claim that the thesis represents the thought of the Reformers, and of its claim to dogmatic truth. For Luther, the principle *sola fide* is inconceivable without previously assumed certainty about Holy Scripture, its reliability, and consequently the historical reality of the history to which it bears witness. This certainty, it is true, is not expressly stated when Luther speaks about faith; it was a wholly self-evident presupposition for Luther, as it was for all his contemporaries. But it is always taken for granted. So Luther cannot be appealed to, when the principle *sola fide* is severed from that presupposition, and when the principle in isolation is turned against the presupposition and it is suggested that *sola fide* demands the removal of historical certainty—as if such a scepticism were the necessary implication of the assurance of faith and the *sola fide* principle. But in its dogmatic content also this thesis is beside the mark. When it speaks of the "removal of the security of faith," that is in truth only a euphemism for the destruction and surrender of the grounds of faith. For its ground is not a "*kerygma*" which has no reference to history, but the *kerygma* in its retrospective relation to history that actually happened, and thus in part its ground is this history itself.

We too say that faith in Jesus Christ must bear the weight of irremovable uncertainty about many things in the history of Jesus. But it can only do so because the figure and history of Jesus is not, in decisive matters, problematical, but historical. I shall deal again with this point in Chapter 7. The faith whose security has been removed in the manner that *kerygma* theology sets out to do, would be faith without foundations. But is a faith

54

which in this sense is without foundations, still faith?[11]

[11] Diem (*Dogmatik*, p. 84, Eng. trans., p. 91) asks Bultmann: "To what does this faith cling, or what does it believe after every kind of historical basis is withdrawn from it?" (and see all that Diem says further in this passage). That Diem arrives at certainty about the history of Jesus by a different route from mine, and that he would probably sharply dissent from the way I indicate in Chapter 7, makes no difference whatever to our agreement in emphasising the question about the historical reality of the history of Jesus.

6

Friedrich Gogarten's Defence of Rudolf Bultmann

IN his book *Entmythologisierung und Kirche*, Friedrich Gogarten attempts to defend Bultmann's thesis that "it is illegitimate to ask whether the traditional material is historically reliable." And yet I am unable to avoid the conclusion that the case he makes entirely misses the real question, and the theological concern of those who are opposed to Bultmann's thesis. In every sentence he writes on this issue Gogarten betrays that he does not take seriously the historical aspect of the *kerygma*. It is theologically illegitimate, he tells us, to ask whether the tradition is reliable, because such an inquiry, carried through consistently, must imply an attempt "to understand the traditional material as part of the context of world events," while in fact "History as it is handed down to us by the *kerygma*, actually becomes present and happens in that act of preaching, and has its peculiar character precisely in this, that it does not spring from the context of world events." Further, we are told, the question of the historical reliability of the traditional material concerns "facts of the past," which the historical investigator—here Bultmann is quoted—"reproduces in their purely empirical character as world events." On the other hand, the past to which belongs the history handed down to us by the *kerygma*, "is not a past on which we can look back as we can on those things which once happened within the context of world events, and now have passed away."[1] Here, it seems to me, two things are persistently confused

[1] Gogarten, *Entmythologisierung und Kirche*, p. 76.

56

and treated as one—first, the saving character of the events handed down to us in *kerygma* (Bultmann's "significance"); and second, the really "empirical" event which faith sees as "saving history." And yet we have here to do with two elements in the "history handed down to us in the *kerygma*." These elements cannot indeed be separated; but for all that they must be distinguished. It is no help, but merely conceals the problem, to declare, as Gogarten does, that "this history is eschatological."[2] Of course it is eschatological, in so far as it is understood by the faith of the first witnesses, and is now proclaimed as such. But its eschatological character is attached to a historical event which unquestionably has an empirical character. And as such this event can and must be remembered and tested to see whether the tradition which reports it is reliable. And in this respect the event does belong to a past "on which we can look back as we can on those things which once happened within the context of world events and now have passed away." How can anyone bring himself to deny this? The events are dated in time and located in space. They do in fact stand in the context of world events and unquestionably, in their historical aspect, can in great part be understood "within the context of world events." Or would it not be a theologically relevant undertaking to investigate the place of the historical event of the cross of Christ within the context of world events? God's act of salvation by the cross is performed through an event which has also a secular aspect, and faith is intensely interested in this aspect because it cannot live on a myth, but depends on actual facts within our history. What else does the Bible mean when it says: "the Word became flesh"? Further, it will not do to say simply of the event handed down to us by the *kerygma*, that the *kerygma* hands down to us the history, which happens and becomes contemporary with us in the act of transmission. This phrase

[2] Ibid.

again conceals the distinction which we emphasised. The history of Jesus, the cross, for example, is in one respect simply an event which has happened, and it does not happen again when the *kerygma* is preached.

Golgotha is not everywhere, but in Jerusalem, and the day of Jesus's death was a particular day. On that day something happened that does not continue, and does not happen when the *kerygma* is preached, but happened once, and once for all.

Gogarten himself goes on to speak of "the historical event of the crucifixion."[3] But he formulates the relation of the "saving event which is the cross of Christ" to the historical event in the strangest and most revealing manner by saying that the former has its temporal origin in the latter, i.e. the event of Golgotha. Only its "temporal origin"? Gogarten here takes over a phrase of Bultmann: "As salvation event thus the cross of Christ is not a mythical occurrence, but an historic event, which takes its origin in the historical occurrence of the crucifixion of Jesus of Nazareth."[4] The expression is of a piece with Bultmann's theology. For in his thought there is no place for the cross of Christ as a saving event as Church doctrine has understood the term; but "Christ's cross and passion are contemporary with us."[5] Bultmann adduces only the passages from the New Testament which treat of our dying with Christ. But the others, such as Rom. III.24ff., or II Cor. v.18, in which it is said that Christ bears vicariously the sin of the world, are held to be "mythological interpretation."[6] Consequently, Christ's death as death *for us* is entirely ignored in favour of our dying *with Him*, in which His cross becomes contemporary with us; and we read: "To believe in the cross of Christ is not to look at a mythical occurrence, which took place outside of us and our world, an objectively visible event which God reckons

[3] *Op. cit.*, p. 77.   [4] Bultmann, *Offenbarung und Heilsgeschehen*, p. 62.
[5] Ibid.   [6] *Op. cit.*, p. 60.

as having happened for our sake. No, to believe in the cross means rather to take Christ's cross upon us as our own, it means to let ourselves be crucified with Christ."[7] As I have said above, here one line of thought in the New Testament is played off against the other; the one is represented as existential, and the other as mythological. And, we may ask with what right, with what standard of judging what is mythological and not mythological? At all events, the description of the historical event on Golgotha as the "origin" of the "historic event"—as Bultmann understands the concept "historic"—is of a piece with his theology. But when we find the phrase in Gogarten, we are startled, and ask ourselves if it is consistent with his doctrine of the cross as he represents it, e.g. in his book *Verhängnis und Hoffnung der Neuzeit*,[8] or in his *Was ist Christentum?*.[9] For there the day of Golgotha is indeed, not only the "temporal origin" of the salvation event, but—if I understand him rightly—a transaction in itself of decisive character between the Father and the Son, which indeed embraces us all, and thus far is contemporary with us, but not in such a manner as to justify the description of the historical happening on Golgotha merely as "origin." "Because the Crucified is He who alone in obedience and in the power of God has taken upon Himself responsibility and lordship in relation to the many, so that which took place between God and Him is at the same time what in Him takes place between God and us." The question is, can Gogarten accept as complete Bultmann's definition of what it means "to believe in the cross"? And would Bultmann accept Gogarten's interpretation in the above-mentioned passages as existential, or does he find mythological ideas even in Gogarten?

[7] *Op. cit.*, p. 61.
[8] Gogarten, *Verhängnis und Hoffnung der Neuzeit*, Stuttgart 1953, pp. 49ff.
[9] Id., *Was ist Christentum?*, Stuttgart 1956, pp. 27ff.

Gogarten declares that for the "true historic event" of Golgotha "between the Crucified and God, there are no historical proofs."[10] Of course not! "For what alone was decisive, what concerns us, happened, if at all, in the obedience, or as we can also say, in the faith of Him who died on the cross." But faith "can be perceived only by faith." Right! The salvation event of Golgotha cannot be "objectively demonstrated" as such. But none of the opponents of Bultmann's thesis has claimed that it could. But the salvation event happens in the element of a historical event. And one must know about the historicity of the latter. Gogarten is continually asserting that with all this knowledge nothing is known about the salvation event as such. Of course not! Nor is that the question on which we differ from him. Rather is it this. Is not the certainty that the event of Golgotha, the death of Jesus on the cross, was historical reality, an essential part of the faith which alone can perceive the salvation event? Does this historicity belong to the things that "concern" faith, and can faith, in obtaining this certainty, dispense with the way of historical verification? In a word: faith confesses that Jesus the Christ (i.e. the mediator between God and man) died as such on the cross. It is decisive that He died as the Christ, for all of us; and faith alone knows this. But it is not less essential for faith that this so-called Christ event is not a myth, but that the real man Jesus died. That is a historical question. Faith cannot declare it a matter of indifference. It cannot undertake to answer it from its own resources. Here it is driven to ask the retrospective historical question. And for this question the gospels, without any detriment to their character as witnesses of faith, must also be considered as historical sources. And the dogmatic theologians only interpose their veto here when they regard certain presuppositions as quite axiomatic, and hold to them like monomaniacs

[10] *Was ist Christentum?*, pp. 27ff.

through thick and thin. As a matter of fact no one ever thinks of doing this in practice. Or are we to believe that in Gogarten's opinion the historical investigation of the gospels as practised by Bultmann, and the resulting verification of the history of Jesus, has no significance for faith? Is it a straying of theology beyond its proper field, which the systematic theologian could pass by without interest?

We must here refute Gogarten's book sentence by sentence. What a misrepresentation it is of the theologian's interest in knowing that the story of Jesus is a story that really happened, when Gogarten first asserts that "the salvation event, the cross of Christ, for example, has its temporal origin in the historical event of the crucifixion of Jesus of Nazareth," and then goes on to say: "But it would imply a desire to rely upon the world and the context of events within it, if we sought within that context for grounds for the trustworthiness of the tradition."[11] An ambiguous sentence! It would be right if its purpose was merely to deny that knowledge about the historical occurrence of Golgotha could give us certainty about the salvation event in the cross of Christ, or could increase our certainty about it. But who believes that? But the sentence is utterly wrong if by using the formula "a desire to rely upon the world," it is trying to declare suspect on theological grounds the historical question about the reliability of the tradition. I can only answer: Yes, indeed, the historical reliability of the story of Jesus in the New Testament narratives is an essential constituent of the basis of faith. The New Testament authors themselves invite us to ask this question (1 Cor. xv.3ff.; Lk. 1.1ff.). We have really to investigate a piece of the world, and rely upon a piece of the world, inasmuch as it has pleased God to give us His salvation event in, with, and under a quite earthly event, which does in fact stand "within the

[11] *Entmythologisierung und Kirche*, p. 77.

context of world events." The historical and mundane reality of Golgotha is the bearer of the salvation event, and the latter is not real unless the former is historical. And therefore we must inquire into the historical reality.

But in what manner? Gogarten continues: "The reliability [of the tradition] which is here the subject of inquiry must be immanent in the tradition, and cannot be given to it from elsewhere. For faith in the *kerygma*, if it really believes in the *kerygma*, can be nothing other than faith in God, faith that it is true to say 'He turned to me His fatherly heart'."[12] But here again the historical moment is left out of account. Faith in Jesus Christ (Gogarten says; in the *kerygma*) includes in itself the certainty that God turned His fatherly heart to us in a definite historical reality. And so one element in the reliability of the tradition is its relationship to historical events; and this distinguishes it from myth, as we know it in other religions, and perhaps also in Mahayana Buddhism. This relation to historical events, i.e. the character of preachers of the gospel as witnesses to an historical event, is not borne in upon us by the mere content of the preaching. Certainty about this relation is not a question of faith in God, but the concern of a retrospecive historical question and reflexion which is something different from an act of faith. When the *kerygma* elicits faith from us, we may not even be explicitly aware of that element in our certainty which concerns the "trustworthiness" of the tradition. In that case faith presupposes the historical trustworthiness of the tradition as something already given. But as soon as faith enters the field where scientific questions and questions of truth are raised, and where consequently critical doubts can arise, the question of historical trustworthiness thrusts itself forward as a problem in its own right and with its own importance, and must be answered by theology as an independent

12 *Entmythologisierung und Kirche*, p. 77.

question. And this has in fact been done ever since theology became a scholarly discipline. The theological work done in the field of introductions to the New Testament is by no means irrelevant to the certainty of faith in the New Testament message, even if the majority of church members are quite ignorant of it. Even an untheological Christian can awaken at any moment to the urgency of the question of historical reliability, and demand an answer. When that happens, then it is not simply the case, as Gogarten affirms, that the tradition bears its own self-authentication. The historical question must receive a historical answer. To use the terms of old dogmatic theology, the witness which the Holy Spirit bears to the truth of the message, cannot extend to a guarantee of its historicity. To claim the contrary would be fanaticism; it would in fact mean that we were not holding fast in our theology to the true humanity, the historicity of Jesus, but seeking to evade the consequent difficulties and distresses to which that humanity exposes us in our search for certainty. The *humanitas* of Christ, i.e. the fact that Jesus has His place in history, and as such, can only be reached through historical tradition and historical witnesses, implies that there is always an element of *fides humana* included in our certainty about the Jesus Christ of the *kerygma*. It certainly must be sharply distinguished from the *fides divina*, the certainty of our faith concerning the presence of God and His salvation in the history to which the *kerygma* bears witness. The *fides humana* can never create the *fides divina*, but the latter is never without the former. This is very inconvenient for the dogmatic theologian, for it implies that there are two components in our religious assurance, and the dogmatic theologian would like to have homogeneity, a monism in the doctrine of the word of God, and in the doctrine of our assurance about it. But this can be attained only at the cost of theologically suppressing the historical element in the concept of the word of God as it is contained in the New Testament, and suppressing with it all the difficulties that it raises for the problems of religious certainty.[13]

I can best make clear my agreement and disagreement with Friedrich Gogarten by reference to his sentences quoted already on p. 40.[14] There he describes Bultmann's and his own conception of history, in contrast with that of the theologians whom he opposes, thus: "The authentic history and . . . historicity of the events to which the New Testament bears witness, is not to be sought in their objective historically ascertainable character as facts that actually happened, but in the *kerygma*, the witness of preaching to the gracious approach which God made in this history to men and to their world." There would be no disagreement between us if instead of "not," Gogarten were to say "not merely," "not alone." For then it would be clear that this real history in Gogarten's sense is *not* real *without* that "objective, historically verifiable character of having actually happened." It is this "not without" which is important. A further sentence in what follows gives me reason to hope that Gogarten will concede the importance of these words "not without," and thereby allow the independent status and the indubitable theological legitimacy of the inquiry about "verifiable historical events." He says: "Our concern with history does not attain its purpose *merely* [my italics] in the investigations which reconstruct and determine the past facts of history." Here these investigations are clearly allowed to have their own legitimate status; indeed Gogarten adds that such investigation is "a means to this understanding." Investigation is thus conceded an independent preparatory significance in relation to "understanding." At an earlier

---

[13] Cf. on this general theme Althaus, *Christliche Wahrheit*, §§ 17, 18; also Kinder in Ellwein, Kinder, and Künneth, *Zur Entmythologisierung*, p. 49, and Künneth in *op. cit.*, p. 80.

[14] Gogarten, *Entmythologisierung und Kirche*, pp. 44ff.

point Gogarten had already stated that, in Bultmann's opinion and in his own, history "is not only a matter of the past," and that the task which it sets us "is thus not exhausted by the investigation which determines what actually objectively happened." Absolutely agreed! None of the theologians whom Bultmann condemns so sharply would differ here. "Is not exhausted," certainly not, but this phrase concedes the point that a concern with history—and thus with the history with which the *kerygma* deals—must also include investigation into what happened, though that is not the only thing we have to do. Here then the admission seems to be made after all that the history which becomes our contemporary in the *kerygma* has a historical dimension in which it belongs to the past, on which we can look back as we can on other events in the past.

Gogarten declares that when the story of Jesus Christ is "dissevered from the preaching" in which alone it has come to us, then the true sense of the history, on which everything depends, is lost.[15] We can answer this with a phrase from Gunther Bornkamm: "The task set us is to seek history in the *kerygma* of the gospels, but also the *kerygma* in the history."[16] Here then the distinction is made between *kerygma* and history, and the inquiry about the "history in the *kerygma*" is stated to be legitimate and conceived as such. But Bornkamm continues as follows: "If we are bidden to make the distinction between them, it is only that we should bring out the more clearly their relationship and their mutual interpenetration." One might exactly describe the relationship of *kerygma* and history by using the four negations of the Chalcedonian formula for the divine humanity of Christ.[17] Here too it is

<hr>

[15] *Entmythologisierung und Kirche*, p. 45.

[16] Bornkamm, *Jesus von Nazareth*, p. 18.

[17] *Translator's note*: The reference here is to the formula concerning Christ adopted by the Council of Chalcedon (A.D. 451): " . . . therefore

true that the two, the *kerygma* and history, are to be *distinguished*—that we are confronted by an indissoluble duality which it is impossible monistically to transcend by blurring the concept of history (*Geschichtlichkeit*). But on the other hand we must hold equally fast to the notion of "mutual interpenetration," since every *separation* is to be avoided.

following the holy fathers we all with one consent teach men to confess one and the same Son, our Lord Jesus Christ . . . to be acknowledged in two natures without confusion, without mutation, without division, without separation (ἀσυγχύτως, ἀτρέπτως, ἀδιαιρέτως, ἀχωρίστως)."

7

The Problem of Certainty
in Historical Knowledge

THUS faith cannot avoid inquiring about the genuine historicity of the story of Jesus Christ, to which the *kerygma* bears witness. And this is a historical undertaking. Then obviously faith finds itself in the old desperate difficulty which has been so often indicated since Lessing's day, the intolerable incongruity between the certainty of faith and the relativity of historical knowledge. When we pass behind the *kerygma*, and ask for its foundation in past history, then faith in Jesus Christ clearly becomes dependent on historical investigation. Does this not make genuine certainty in faith absolutely impossible? (We saw this question also in Martin Kähler.) Faith possesses the character of absolute certainty, but historical knowledge is always relative, never absolute, always only approximately sure, of greater or less probability: the degree of approximation may be very high, but it never reaches absolute certainty. Further, only the expert trained investigator can pass authoritative historical judgments. The others, who are "laymen" in history, have no independent judgment of their own; they are forced to rely on the authority of the investigators; their confidence in the story of Jesus, and consequently their faith in Jesus Christ, has the character of faith in the authority of others. And that means an end to the claim that each individual can have immediate faith in God and knowledge of Him. The universal priesthood is negated at this decisive point, and a papacy of the scholars set up; between Jesus Christ and the Christian there stands no longer the priest, but the professor—the unlettered man is degraded again to the position of a "layman" in the central point of his Christian status. Can Protestant Christianity let itself in for this without surrendering its key position? What remains of the status and freedom of every Protestant Christian, if the ground of his faith in Jesus Christ is no longer immediately accessible, and he is to be dependent on the mediation of the historians? What then distinguishes the Protestant Christian from the Roman Catholic, whose certainty about Jesus Christ is conditioned by his acknowledgment of the authority of the Church and its teaching office? The incongruity between the knowledge of faith and historical knowledge can be further expressed thus; historical knowledge is achieved through the continually fluctuating results of research; even on matters of practical and vital importance the judgments of historians differ and diverge, while faith demands freedom from ambiguity. Historical knowledge has always an element of the provisional, it is fundamentally inconclusive, because the possibility is never excluded that the discovery of new sources might demand a correction of the hitherto accepted picture. This element of reserve is greater in some cases, less in others; in certain instances it may be reduced to vanishing point, and the records may to all intents and purposes be closed, yet in principle the reservation remains, the possibility of a critical revision of the accepted picture of a past event cannot be excluded. But faith, on the other hand, has the character of final certainty. In face of all these facts, how can we base our faith in Christ on history and on historical judgments?

Bultmann writes: "It is essential to the tradition of the *kerygma* that no questions about the historical trustworthiness of the traditional material be allowed. Otherwise the eschatological event of which the *kerygma* speaks would be drawn into the relativity of all historical knowledge."[1] This means that to preserve the certainty of our faith we must not ask questions about the reliability of the material handed down to us in the *kerygma*, since certainty cannot be attained in this manner.

Is this really the case? And are therefore all retrospective questions about the history on which the *kerygma* is based, to be repudiated as incompatible with faith? No, the truth is not so simple as this. The sentences quoted above on the relation of the certainty of faith and our arrival at certainty about historical facts, are in this form quite abstract, and do not do justice to the variety of elements within our knowledge of history. Even a theory of general historical knowledge carries us beyond Bultmann's position.[2] It is not in fact, correct to say that all our relationship to past history and our knowledge of it is exclusively mediated through inductive work of the historian on the sources. Even the scholarly historian does not use these resources alone. He too requires "intuition," an imaginative "encounter" with the past piece of life, and this intuition goes along with his inductive research and has a strong influence on his historical judgments as to what is genuine and what false. "Encounter" means that there is an immediate pre-scientific relationship to past history, spanning centuries and millennia, which carries in itself absolute certainty about this past life. In such encounter we know whether tradition is genuine. It is here exactly the same as in our encounter with contemporary life. Our certainty about the character of another man is not bound to the empirical inductive method. That is, it is not necessary for me first to have had long practical experience of another man, or to have psycho-analysed him before I know about him. At my

[1] *Kerygma und Mythos*, VOL. I, p. 147.
[2] For the following see my *Grundriss der Dogmatik*, VOL. I, § 9.3.

first encounter I can reach an immediate conclusion about him, which can give me unshakable confidence in him. The immediacy in our knowledge of past life is exactly analogous. Admittedly, in order to have such knowledge we must have a relation to the subject, the centre of that past life. The man who himself has a vital concern for the truth, the question of the true meaning of the Gospel, will know also the decisive things about Luther, and will know him in every point, even in his errors and mistakes, as one devoted to this concern; and will know that Dénifle's or even Grisar's reading of his character and motives miss the point.

Such an immediate encounter, in the case of past life as also in the case of our contemporaries, must of course seek continually to verify its results by means of inductive historical scholarship, in its detailed work of the evaluation of the sources. The encounter, in fact, gives certainty to our judgments only on large issues, not on points of detail. It can give assurance about the genuineness of tradition in essentials, in fundamentals; it cannot guarantee the historicity of all the individual particulars. The general conclusions are absolutely certain, but many separate and isolated points may be questionable and matter of debate. Here, consequently, our knowledge of past history has in it a tension between the certainty which arises in the encounter, and the uncertainty of historical work on details. Here those contrasts which we mentioned above— between the certainty of faith and the certainty of historical knowledge—do exist, but their place is not between faith and history, but within historical knowledge itself. The certainty which springs from the encounter must always be content to suffer the pressure and the questionings of scientific historical criticism, whose results in principle never attain to conclusive certainty. Here also the analogy with our knowledge of contemporary life holds good; even my certainty about the character of a man to whom I am bound by loyalty, can be called in question by painful experiences, and questioning must continually be overcome by renewal of trust.

All this means that our relation to past history is not solely and entirely mediated through historical scholarship and its methods, but is established first and foremost in the immediate encounter of our mind with the past piece of life. But such an immediate encounter stands in an ineradicable tension with the essentially inconclusive character of scientific historical knowledge, and must be content to abide in that tension.

These insights into a general theory of historical knowledge hold good also for our knowledge of the story of Jesus, and in particular for our conception of His person. Be it noted in passing that if anyone wishes to raise theological objections to our taking knowledge of the story of Jesus as a particular case of historical knowledge, and discussing it within the framework of general propositions of historical epistemology; if anyone here, where historical certainty not faith is the theme, wishes for, or himself sets up, a special theological epistemology, he had better ask himself whether he is taking seriously the true humanity of our Lord, and the fully historical character of His manifestation. For this implies that Jesus Christ, in the matter of His historical character as such, occupies no privileged sacral position, but entered fully into the realm of historical reality, and was content both to live and to be known under the principles obtaining in that sphere. Thus knowledge of Him as an historical reality is conditioned fundamentally by the same principles as historical knowledge elsewhere and in general.

If, with these ideas in mind, we turn to the question of our knowledge of Jesus and His story, we find that all these antitheses between the certainty of faith and the merely probable, uncertain, and mediate character of historical knowledge receive fresh force; when we consider, that is, the researches of the historical critics into the life of Jesus, their formulations of the problem, and their results. Here too there is a continual fluctuation, and over large areas a diversity of opinions and a conflict of results among the several investigators; but everywhere the realisation, so depressing for faith, that we must draw a distinction between primary and secondary tradition. And we must admit that the latter has been shaped by apologetic and dogmatic considerations, and consequently has legendary features. We find too that the boundary between historically "genuine" and "fictitious" words of Jesus is uncertain and fluid, that the Christology of primitive Christendom in many points modified the words of Jesus, and added alien elements to them, indeed—as the problem of the sayings of Jesus in John's gospel shows us—largely transformed them. And so we must acknowledge that in the words which the New Testament puts in Jesus's mouth, problems, questions and answers of the later Church in which Matthew, Luke, and John lived, have left their traces.[3] And where in all this is there a firm foundation for the theological layman, the non-specialist who is seeking for a foundation of his faith in Christ?

And yet all the above-named results and undecided questions of the researches of the historical critics have in no way blurred the characteristic features of the person and the story of Jesus. We must not let our gaze be confused by the dust which research has raised in the foreground, but we must attempt to see through it. It was customary a generation ago, especially under the influence of Albert Schweitzer's *Quest of the Historical Jesus*, to use strong expressions about the impossibility of knowing either the person of Jesus or His story. Bultmann declares "that we can today know practically nothing of the life and personality of Jesus."[4] Such a statement is under-

[3] Cf. my *Christliche Wahrheit*, § 15.
[4] Bultmann, *Jesus*, p. 12.

72

standable as a repudiation of the Life-of-Jesus literature of the nineteenth century, with its psychological interest in Jesus's "personality," and its attempt to write the Life of Jesus pragmatically as a biography. But, taken out of this context, the thesis represents an intolerable exaggeration. Today, when it is advocated, it frequently serves to represent the inquiry into the historical background and foundation of the *kerygma* as hopeless and insoluble, and thus to justify the isolation of the apostolic preaching from what preceded it. Luckily, in the actual representations of Jesus, e.g. in Bultmann's own book, the soup is not eaten so hot as it was cooked when the general principles were enunciated.

Both in his book on Jesus and in his *Theologie des Neuen Testaments*, Bultmann gives an account of Jesus's preaching; but do we not also find *Him*, His personal outlook, in His preaching? And conversely is His outlook, about which we can know a great deal, in spite of all our critical reservations in respect of the primitive Christian sources, not itself a part of His "preaching"? It is impossible to keep Jesus's teaching and Himself apart—and even Bultmann does not seriously try to do so.

Martin Kähler is right; the impossibility of inventing the fundamental features of the New Testament picture of Christ in its concreteness is the immediate and inevitable conclusion which thrusts itself on the unprejudiced student. These fundamental features of His outlook, like the fundamental thoughts of His message, have been preserved through every layer of the tradition; His humility under God, and, inseparably conjoined with it, His claim to divinely given authority and His exercise of it; His dedication to the purposes of the Father, and in the same breath His dedication to the service of man; the radical seriousness of His challenge; His verdicts, His judgments of men's hearts—and His limitless and unconditional forgiveness of the guilty; His turning towards the needy,

73

the poor, the sinners; His certainty that God's hour for them had struck—these are some of the characteristics that persistently and everywhere meet us in the tradition about Him. It is these which make Him everywhere recognisable. They are no wish-fulfilment created by the human longing for a Saviour, the reports about them are too concrete and individual for that; the picture of Jesus contradicts all expectation, shocks, and gives offence, an offence which the later texts seek to alleviate, and even to remove. The decisive characteristics of the outlook and words of Jesus make themselves felt even in the secondary traditional material, e.g. in the gospel of John. Thus the boundary between what is supposed to be historically genuine and original, and secondary and later, and the impossibility of everywhere drawing a clear line of demarcation between them, becomes here relatively unimportant. Jesus and His character have left their stamp deeply on the secondary, even on the legendary material. When we consider the whole we find a consensus in the tradition about the fundamental characteristics, which persists throughout all the manifold accommodations, developments and adjustments of the material. So we can distinguish between authenticity in the historical sense of the *verba ipsissima* and the exact historicity of the narratives on the one hand, and authenticity of content on the other. And that which is inauthentic in the first sense often turns out to be authentic in the second.

Or are we with all these statements introducing a harmony which belies the real situation in scholarly research? Are the investigators not of thoroughly different opinions, for example, on the issue whether Jesus regarded Himself as the Messiah, i.e. the Christ, or the Son of Man?[5] But these questions do not place in dispute the clarity of the fundamental characteristics of Jesus. What does it matter

[5] See the discussion on this point in Bornkamm, *Jesus von Nazareth*, and E. Stauffer, *Jesus: Gestalt und Geschichte*, Bern 1957.

whether we answer these questions with "Yes" or "No,"
when all who judge differently here, are at one in this,
that Jesus was sure "that men's fate depended on their
relation to Him"?[6] The concept of the Messiah or of the
Son of Man would in any case only be the form in which
this claim of Jesus found expression. But the content of
the claim is not tied to the appropriation of the titles,
and consequently the knowledge of Christ's claim to
authority is not dependent on a unanimous judgment that
He applied one or both of these titles to Himself.

The genuine historicity of the picture of Jesus in its
fundamental characteristics forces itself upon every one
that lives with the picture. It is not necessary to be a
scholar to get this impression. It is pre-scientific. The
"layman" is not here dependent on the authority of the
theologian. Rather is it true to say that even the theologian, the theological historian, can only bear witness to
this impression and express it.

Thus G. Bornkamm writes: "The gospels bring the
historical figure of Jesus before us in the immediacy of His
power. Too clear is the report which the gospels give us
of Jesus's message, His deeds and His story, still today
marked by an authenticity, a freshness and an individuality
not subdued even by the Easter faith of the Church, which
carry us directly back to the earthly figure of Jesus."[7] It
is indeed impossible to write a biographical or psychological life of Jesus, "and yet the gospels give us no excuse
for resignation or scepticism." The historian is compelled
to criticise the gospel tradition which "not seldom blurs
the distinction between history and interpretation. And
yet we must not let ourselves be blinded to the fact that
in, with, and under just this method of tradition and
narrative the figure and the influence of Jesus in unmistakable uniqueness and singularity are made visible with

[6] Bultmann, *Theologie des Neuen Testaments*, p. 26.
[7] Bornkamm, *Jesus von Nazareth*, p. 21.

an originality which ever and again far transcends and disarms the understanding of the believer and his powers of interpretation. Thus understood the primitive Christian tradition about Jesus is filled to the brim with history."[8] In detail Bornkamm shows how, for example, "the astonishing sovereignty of Jesus with which He masters the situation in different ways according to the different character of the men who encounter Him" is shown again and again in very many different narratives, and even in some which belong to the legendary material of tradition. The essential point is, that in all of them, this same characteristic recurs, by which the historical Jesus can be recognised.[9] Bornkamm comes from the school of Bultmann; but the alteration in tone is unmistakable compared with that sceptical sentence from Bultmann's *Jesus*. In Bornkamm there speaks, in spite of all, a much stronger confidence in the essential trustworthiness of the tradition, the confidence that we can recognise "the historical figure of Jesus." A striking difference between the two books on Jesus is that, although they both bear the same title, Bultmann confines himself to giving an account of Jesus's preaching; the word appears in the title of the three chief chapters. But in Bornkamm's book we find one special section, which precedes the account of the preaching of Jesus, entitled "Jesus of Nazareth." In Bultmann we read, let me quote it once again: "I am of the opinion that we can know practically nothing of the life and personality of Jesus."[10] But in Bornkamm: "The nature of the sources forbids us to depict Jesus's story biographically against the background of the history of His people and His time. And yet, the historical material which the sources give us for the person and career of Jesus is not so negligible, and must be taken carefully into account."[11] The difference is evident. For Bultmann the search for the "historical

[8] Bornkamm, *Jesus von Nazareth*, p. 23.　　　[9] *Op. cit.*, p. 23f.
[10] Bultmann, *Jesus*, p. 12.　　[11] Bornkamm, *Jesus von Nazareth*, p. 48.

Jesus" is theologically forbidden, for Bornkamm it is not only permitted, but enjoined.[12]

At the risk of tedium let me repeat once more that our interest in the possibility of knowing the decisive characteristics of Jesus's person and His history has nothing to do with an attempt to give an apologetic "underpinning" to faith in Jesus Christ, and thereby to take from it the character of faith, putting in its place a demonstrable knowledge about the revelation, the "Divinity of Christ." There is no thought of this. The revelation, the presence of God in Jesus Christ is known only in faith. It cannot be cogently deduced from the historical facts as such. But faith, though unquestionably the miracle of the Holy Spirit, arises none the less in relation to witnessed history, and not least in relation to the picture of Jesus, as it shows itself "undisguised and underivable, prior to every interpretation by faith."[13] As W. Mundle says, with reference to the question of the resurrection of Jesus from the empty tomb, and His appearances, we can call the reality of Jesus to which the gospel bears witness, "signs" which are given to faith, signs which give us an indication, but do not remove a man's responsibility for decision, but rather call him to it.[14] But even if the historical facts in this sense are only "signs," faith is still absolutely interested in the reality of the "signs."

The impression of the historical reality of the figure of Jesus is not imparted only to the believer in Jesus Christ. Thus we see the matter differently from Wilhelm Herrman.[15] He too speaks of the impression that the New Testament picture of Jesus is authentic, and could not

---

[12] Bornkamn, *Jesus von Nazareth*, p. 20.

[13] *Op. cit.*, p. 48.

[14] W. Mundle, *Der Glaube an Christus und der historische Zweifel*, Metzingen 1950, p. 101.

[15] *Der Verkehr des Christen mit Gott*, 5th and 6th edns. Stuttgart and Berlin 1908, pp. 59ff.; id., *Dogmatik*, Gotha and Stuttgart 1925, pp. 28ff.

77

have been invented. But he ties this impression to our religious experience in relation to this picture. "When the person of Jesus as we can apprehend it in the New Testament becomes for us the pure manifestation of the power which we can only call God, because it alone wholly subjugates us . . . when this one gift is given us through the New Testament picture of Jesus which we have apprehended, then we are no longer able to conceive of this picture as a poem created by man." "Thus the person of Jesus becomes a power that really stands in history, not by means of historical proofs, but through our experience of the picture of the spiritual life of Jesus . . . If we experience in relation to it what we elsewhere seek in vain, the vision of the only One to whom we can wholly surrender ourselves in dedication, then we cannot any more free ourselves from our subjugation to Him. This we would however try to do, if we were able to see that picture as the creation of human fantasy. For then we could in principle have confidence that we could create such a picture from the means at our own disposal. And thus the absolute subjugation to that which here confronts us would be at an end." These statements will not do. It is not only the experience of God and His salvation in the person of Jesus which makes us certain of His historical reality, but "reason" itself, if we understand it as openness for reality and as the power to distinguish it from a picture of fantasy. We are not now inquiring whether too much is being demanded of our experience of salvation through Christ, when to it alone is ascribed the knowledge that the picture of Jesus could not have been invented. (Karl Heim has with justice objected that this is so.)[16] But our opinion is, that our "Yes" to the message about Jesus Christ includes a rational judgment, that is an impression of such reality in the figure and essential characteristics of the story of Jesus as

[16] Karl Heim, *Leitfaden der Dogmatik*, 3rd edn. Halle 1923, VOL. I, p. 49.

is beyond the power of invention. And this is a judgment which is possible even for the unbeliever, and which, as experience shows us, he is constantly making, consciously or unconsciously.

The believer himself, so long as he does not reflect theologically, does not distinguish this moment of "rational" certainty included in his affirmation of the message, from the certainty which his faith possesses as to the presence of God and His salvation in Jesus Christ. But theological reflexion singles this out as a distinct factor, and brings it to consciousness. It asks also the critical question as to the ground and justification of the judgment of "reason," just as it does in the case of faith's certainty about the presence of God. In any case the former is independent of the latter. The former we share with every man who, with whatever intentions, concerns himself with the person and story of Jesus in the narratives which tell of it: the latter is the concern of the Church alone, and distinguishes it from all other communities.

The significance of Bornkamm's new book on Jesus lies not least in this, that it in fact distinguishes clearly and expressly, even if not in a systematic and reflected manner, the two judgments and the two certainties, and does not regard either of them as given along with the other. He speaks of an "immediate authority" with which the historical figure of Jesus imposes itself upon us, independent of all "believing comprehension and interpretation." In fact neither can faith in the salvation event itself decide the question of historicity, nor on the other hand can historical confidence as such give us the knowledge of faith.

8

On Bultmann's Existential Christology

IN his essay on the Christological Confession of the World
Council of Churches 1951-2, with reference to the
titles given to Jesus in the New Testament, Bultmann
says: "The decisive question would appear to be how far
the different titles intend to say something about the
nature of Jesus, how far, so to speak, they describe Him
in an objectifying manner as He is in Himself, or whether
and how far they speak of Him in His significance for man,
for faith. Do they speak of a φύσις or do they speak of the
Christus pro me? How far is a Christological utterance about
Him at the same time an utterance about me? Does He
help me because He is the Son of God, or is He the Son
of God because He helps me?"[1] The last sentence corresponds exactly to the sentence about Christ's cross: "It is
not the salvation event because it is the cross of Christ,
but because it is the salvation event it is the cross of Christ."[2]

Let us try to make clear to ourselves the meaning of
these strange alternatives, this massive "either-or"
(H. Diem). Bultmann contrasts "Jesus as He is in Himself" on the one side, and "His significance for man" on
the other. The concept of "significance" plays a decisive
role in his theology. Thus we are also told, for example,
that the message of the resurrection of Christ can be
nothing other "than the expression of the significance of

---

[1] Bultmann, *Glauben und Verstehen*, VOL. II, pp. 246ff., esp. p. 252.
[2] Bultmann, *Kerygma und Mythos*, VOL. I, p. 5. Cf. *Offenbarung und Heilsgeschehen*, p. 62f.

the cross."[3] If every statement about Christ deals only with His "significance for man," then every statement about the being of Christ is excluded which is not at the same time a statement about me. Any such statement not related to my existence would then be an expression of "objectifying Greek thought,"[4] would be entangled in the subject-object mode of thinking, which has been super- seded by truly historic (*geschichtlich*) thinking. The old Greek doctrine of Christ was framed by this objectifying thought, and is therefore for us out of date. This is precisely what we hear from Gogarten. He too contrasts the "*metaphysical* interpretation of Christian faith" "as it received its classical form in the Christological and Trinitarian dogma of the ancient Church," with the *historic* interpretation of the Christian faith which is the only possible one for us.[5] "Thus it is no longer possible for theology to revive the metaphysical interpretation, as it found its classical form in the dogma of the ancient Church. . . . If accordingly the metaphysical interpreta- tion of faith has been made impossible by historic think- ing, then theology today can only interpret faith historic- ally (*geschichtlich*)."[6] Accordingly Gogarten too rejects the subject-object mode of thinking, and, in face of the critics, defends Bultmann's talk about "significance" as the decisive category for the interpretation which faith must offer of the story of Jesus.[7]

[3] Bultmann, *Offenbarung und Heilsgeschehen*, p. 63.
[4] Bultmann, *Glauben und Verstehen*, VOL. II, p. 257.
Translator's note: "Objectifying thought" (*objektivierendes Denken*). It is hard to find any suitable English equivalent for this term in Bultmann. By it he wishes to describe a mode of thinking like that of science, which sets out to deal with the world of objects coolly and without passion—a type of thinking entirely legitimate in dealing with the empirical world, but wholly out of place in the realm of faith. Objectifying thought is, it need hardly be pointed out, both for Bultmann and for Gogarten, the same as the subject-object mode of thinking.
[5] Gogarten, *Entmythologisierung und Kirche*, pp. 33ff.   [6] *Op. cit.*, p. 43f.
[7] *Op. cit.*, pp. 95ff. I cannot deal here in detail with the difference which I think I see between Bultmann and Gogarten on the question of Christology

Bultmann's "either-or" is most sharply expressed in the question: "Does Christ help me because He is the Son of God, or is He the Son of God because He helps me?" Bultmann of course favours the latter alternative. This "either-or" means that faith, and consequently ˌtheology also, has nothing else to say of Jesus than what He does for me, nothing beyond the help He gives for my existence, nothing about *Christus in se*, but only *quoad nos*. Thus Bultmann interprets also Paul's Christology; he actually describes the apostle's teaching on justification as his real Christology.[8] This means that Christology does not consist of speculation about natures, but in the preaching of the Christ event, and is therefore reflexion about oneself, a thinking-through of one's own existence. In Paul the doctrine is "preaching of the Christ event as address, and as its explanation the unfolding of the Christian self-understanding. The titles of Jesus in the New Testament, taken in their proper sense, are not statements, not descriptions, but confessions."[9]

Certainly "confessions"—we too say this. But the question remains whether Bultmann has not formulated a wholly untenable "either-or."

Hermann Diem passes this judgment on the antithesis which Bultmann sets up between correct Christological and false "objectifying" thinking, with special reference to the statement about the divinity of the man Jesus Christ: "This example strikingly illustrates the fact that with a massive alternative, a relentless '*either or*'—e.g. *either* 'nature of Christ' *or* 'Christ *pro me*,' *either* 'metaphysical being' *or* 'significance for the world,' *either* 'objectification in a past event' *or* 'actualisation in the present event of preaching'—all those theological differences which

(see *op. cit.*, p. 70, on the unity between God and Jesus). Would not Bultmann reject the ideas which Gogarten here enunciates, as talk about Jesus as He is in Himself?

[8] Bultmann, *Glauben und Verstehen*, VOL. I, p. 262f.

[9] *Op. cit.*, p. 267.

have agitated the Church throughout the formation of its doctrine can, as it were, be flattened out and the totality of dogmatic statements be relegated to the sphere of metaphysics, as if in the case of each of these stark alternatives there might not also be, starting from the New Testament period itself, a *both-and*."[10]

We too are against "speculations about natures" in theology. But are we also to veto statements about being which express more than Jesus's significance for me? That would certainly be to shut up theology in an existentialist prison. Albrecht Ritschl's "value judgments" have come back in a new form, on the basis of a different philosophy. The much misunderstood and erroneous expression "value judgments" was intended by Ritschl to mean that religious judgments come into existence only in value-experiences, and that accordingly God is only known when we are aware of the *value* of His saving work for our blessedness. Even the predicate of the divinity of Christ is a value judgment, i.e. it signifies the saving value of Christ for us.

"If Christ is my Lord because of what He has done and suffered for my salvation and if I honour Him as my God, by trusting for my salvation to the power of His saving work, that is a value judgment of a direct kind. The judgment does not fall within the territory of cold-blooded scholarly knowledge, like the Chalcedonian formula.... All religious knowledge consists of direct value judgments. What God is, and what the divine is, we can only know in its essence by ascertaining its value for our salvation."[11] Ritschl speaks of "value for salvation," Bultmann of "significance for man." The kinship is unmistakable.[12]

That the expression "value judgments" was unfor-

---

[10] Diem, *Dogmatik*, p. 72, Eng. trans., pp. 77-8.

[11] A. Ritschl, *Rechtfertigung und Versöhnung*, 4th edn. Bonn 1910, VOL. III, §§ 28-44, esp. p. 376.

[12] Cf. also Kinder in *Zur Entmythologisierung*, p. 47, n.9.

tunate, goes without saying. But the fact must not be overlooked that, though he expressed himself wrongly, Ritschl's intention was to distinguish the knowledge of faith from theoretical judgments, such as are used in science; he never wished to deny that they also lay hold on a reality, and thus far are "judgments about being." His mistake was that he wished to measure and limit this reality by the standard of what our human need of salvation recognises as "value for salvation." Similarly we must not, as E. Kinder does, describe Bultmann's existentialism in these words: "Exiled from the dimension of being, these theological statements live their life in the 'flatland' of mere value."[13] We ought not to oppose the "significance" of Bultmann's terminology to "being." He also is concerned with a "being" of Jesus Christ. His mistake is that he limits it to the statement that Christ gives me a new self-understanding (and, consequently, a new being): thus he interprets it inadequately, because anthropologically.

A Christology which confines itself to statements about Jesus Christ, which are at the same time utterances about myself, only "thinking out the implications of my own existence," comes at any rate far short of the Christology of the New Testament. It does so principally in the following respects.

(1) The New Testament sees Jesus not only in His relation to us men who stand in need of salvation, but also in His relation to the *Father*. It speaks of the loving communion between the Father and the Son. In this consists the glory of the Son, which distinguishes Him from all other men (Jn. xvii.5.). And because of this the worship is due to Him which is accorded to Him continually in the prayers of the primitive Christian community. If we take Bultmann's "either-or"—"Does He help me because He is the Son of God, or is He the Son of God

[13] *Zur Entmythologisierung*, p. 37.

because He helps me"—the New Testament certainly affirms the first alternative. Jesus's sonship is more than His help for me, and is not known only through it.

(2) In the same way, in the New Testament, the Easter event has a richer content than the fact that it is the foundation of the Easter faith. In Bultmann the Easter event is reduced to the rise of the Easter faith of the disciples, and consequently to the rise of the gospel, "Christ rises into the word, into the *kerygma*"—thus E. Ellwein summarises Bultmann[14]—and the Easter faith is nothing but faith in the word of preaching. "Jesus Christ, the crucified and risen, meets us in the word of preaching, and nowhere else. Faith in this word is in truth the Easter faith."[15] But the Easter faith for Bultmann is reduced to faith in justification. Now it is certainly correct to say that for Paul faith in justification is the Easter faith (Rom. iv.25.); but the converse that the Easter faith is nothing but faith in justification, is certainly not true. Hans Grass says rightly: "God's revelatory action [at Easter] did not confine itself to the disciples, to the creation of their visions and their faith. But in these visions and in this faith is implied *that God also and indeed in the first place did something to Christ*."[16] And he asks: "Is the living Lord a reality for Bultmann, or is only the *kerygma* a reality, so that in the place of the formula 'cross and resurrection' we ought to put the formula 'cross and *kerygma*'?" For the New Testament more happened at Easter than merely an illumination of the disciples, by means of which they now understood the meaning, the "significance of the cross." There happened in fact *the exaltation of Christ*. He manifests Himself to them in His new exalted life, He gives them grounds for their certainty of His continuing presence and His position as "Lord," and justifies their

---

[14] Ellwein in *Zur Entmythologisierung*, p. 24.
[15] Bultmann, *Offenbarung und Heilsgeschehen*, p. 66.
[16] H. Grass, *Ostergeschehen und Osterberichte*, Göttingen 1956, p. 244 and n.

worship of Him. God dealt certainly with us through Christ at Easter, but first of all He dealt with Christ.

(3) Accordingly, Jesus's position as "Lord" in the New Testament is not confined to His relation *quoad me, pro me,* but transcends it. Bultmann connects Christ's Lordship and His "significance" for me so closely that Christ's Lordship is wholly actualised. "Christ's Lordship, His divinity is always event, and nothing but event."[17] There could be no clearer expression of the fact that for Bultmann Christ's Lordship, His divinity remains wholly within the anthropocentric limits of the relationship to my spiritual existence. In the New Testament the Lordship of Jesus Christ shows itself also in the healing of physical distress. It is not only—as it is even in Ritschl—spiritual Lordship, but authority over the demons and dominion over death, authority to bring in the new world which is promised and which is symbolised by the healing miracles. The meaning of Easter is not only in His manifestation of Himself to the disciples, but is, quite apart from any manifestation, *in itself* a victory over death; the breaking-in of the world of glory in the person of Jesus Christ. The New Testament here makes all manner of judgments of reality, which are not at the same time utterances about human existence. At any rate they are not that first and foremost, but only indirectly, by virtue of Jesus being the first-born from the dead, and possessing many brethren. The Christological content of Easter is independent of its relation to our existence, and prior to it.

The difference between the New Testament's understanding of the Lordship of Christ and that represented by Bultmann, shows itself also in this; in view of the resurrection of Christ, the New Testament looks for a new world; the hope of the Church has cosmic dimentions But Bultmann does not allow himself any eschatological utterances about the redemption of creation and a new

[17] Bultmann, *Glauben und Verstehen*, VOL. II, p. 258.

world, such as we have in Rom. VIII. "These are in fact mythological speculations about the future."[18] In this theology, bound as it is to existential philosophy, the re-creation of the world by God is limited to a new *understanding* of the world, which is received by the believer. But there is no word of a new world; here every statement is declared impossible for theology. "I can indeed understand that people say 'Creation has been made new by God,' in so far as the believer can understand this world, which has fallen a prey to transience, this history of humanity so troubled by sin, once more as God's creation, as God's wonderfully guided history. But I am absolutely unable to form any picture of an end to the process of nature, and an end of history."[19]

On which we might make the comment that the question is not whether we are able "to form a picture"— of what content of faith could we do this?—but whether the thought necessarily belongs to the hope of Christendom which Christ has established.

On these three points mentioned above the New Testament goes beyond what in Bultmann's opinion is the content of Christology. And now the question is, do we have the hardihood to treat the balance, the "plus" of New Testament Christology, as mythology—"to be interpreted existentially"—or whether we are not here brought up against the limits of existential interpretation as the systematic principle of hermeneutics, and see ourselves challenged to break free theologically from the restrictions philosophically imposed upon us by the existential approach. Theologically here we must say, a sharp distinction must be drawn between the *way* of knowing Christ and the *content* of this knowledge. I certainly know Jesus Christ first in His relation to my existence: in that I know

[18] Bultmann, *Die Christliche Hoffnung und das Problem der Entmythologisierung*, Stuttgart 1954, p. 57.
[19] *Op. cit.*, p. 57f.

myself to be judged and blessed when I hear the witness to Him.

But *what* I then know of Him, when I surrender to the witness, far transcends this relation. He is not only the "Word" of God for me. The concept "word" is today often used to confine affirmations about Christ wholly within the relationship to my existence, as is true of the concept "word" when we use it of "address." But Jesus is not only "word"; He is also "the Son"; and in this title the primary thing is not His relationship to us, but His nature "in itself"—that is, His relation to the Father. To be consistent, a Christology which remains within the limits of the existential relation would have to treat the concept "Son" as mythological. Does it really wish to do so?

In this matter we will have to agree with Karl Barth's criticism of Bultmann: "Is it true that we can affirm a theological statement as true when, and only when, it can prove itself to be a genuine constituent of the Christian understanding of human existence? . . . None of the chief articles of the Christian creed fulfil this condition. It is true that they relate to human existence. They make possible and establish the Christian understanding of man. And thus, in changed form, they become also descriptions of human existence. But they do not have this character in the first place. In the first place, they describe the being and actions of the God who is *different* from man, who *meets* man, the Father, the Son, the Holy Spirit. They are therefore not to be reduced to statements about the inner life of man. The anthropological corner into which Bultmann drives systematic theology, and also, unfortunately, exegetical theology, is an inheritance from W. Herrmann, and also, more remotely, from A. Ritschl and Schleiermacher. . . ."[20]

To me it appears indisputable that Bultmann's "exis-

[20] Barth, *Kirchliche Dogmatik*, VOL. III, PT II, p. 535.

tential interpetation" excludes essential material of the New Testament message, material which belongs to its substance, and thus involves a loss of theological substance. Existential interpretation is *one* hermeneutical principle. It has its justification, if it remains conscious of this limitation, and does not make absolutistic pretensions to be the only theological method. Under no circumstances is it legitimate to decree that what cannot be existentially interpreted, i.e. what cannot at the same time be interpreted as an utterance about my own existence, is "mythological." God's kingdom is not confined to the healing of the distresses of human existence. The breaking in of the reign of God is indeed the salvation of man. But the sovereignty of God is an independent theme, which must not be forced within the narrow confines of anthropology. . . .[21]

[21] *Translator's note*: A brief note on Gloege follows in the German text, which has been omitted from the translation as it adds nothing to the argument.